PIRATES AND PATHFINDERS

PIRATES AND PATHFINDERS

BY

MARJORIE W. HAMILTON

Maurice Cody Public School
Critic Teacher, Toronto Normal School

ILLUSTRATIONS AND MAPS BY

JOCELYN TAYLOR

Toronto
CLARKE, IRWIN & COMPANY LIMITED
1947

Printed in Canada

TO THOSE WHO READ THIS BOOK

Pirates and Pathfinders tells the story of some men who have added to the map of the world. It ranges in time from the days of the Norse sea rovers who ventured forth on unknown seas in their tiny sailing ships, to the time of Admiral Byrd who has travelled by land, sea and air from the North Pole to the South Pole. In all ages explorers have journeyed to the far corners of the earth, America, Africa, Australia, the islands of the South Seas, the Arctic and the Antarctic, and have returned to their own land, adding new names of lands, rivers, lakes, islands and seas to the map of the world. It is hoped that the boys and girls who read this book will relive the journeys taken by these adventure-loving men.

The illustrations in this book are part of the story, telling dramatic incidents more vividly than mere words. From these sketches the reader will find out much about the new lands which the explorers discovered. For example, in the sketch of Cook on the Island of Tahiti he will see what sort of people lived on that tropical island, the clothing the people wore, the homes in which they lived and the kind of trees that grew there. The routes taken by the explorers and the places that they visited can be followed on simple maps on which only the places necessary for a better understanding of the story have been marked.

At the end of each story or series of stories, there is a short test, based on the reading material. Its purpose is to enable the reader to check his own learning. The section *Things To Do Together* has been planned for classroom projects. Boys and girls will work together writing letters and diaries, making murals and wall-maps, planning models of ships and villages, preparing plays, and engaging in enterprises of a similar nature. These suggested activities will prove only a beginning for the versatile teacher. *Things To Do Separately* is intended for the pupil interested in further research in a topic. For the most part, the projects here suggested will be carried on outside the classroom.

In the last section, *Books to Read,* there are two lists of suggested readings, one for the pupil and one for the teacher. Here are listed names of books that might well make the basis of a Social Studies library in the classroom.

The majority of the suggested activities at the end of each section have **actually** been tested in the classroom, by the author. At all times during the preparation of the book, the author has kept in mind its practical use in school.

There are still regions of the world about which little is known. The world, even yet, needs pathfinders to go out with determination and courage and bring back new knowledge. We may not all be explorers; but if we understand more fully what others have done for us in the past, and if we know more about the peoples and lands visited by these men, then we shall be better fitted to live in peace and harmony with one another in One World.

MARJORIE W. HAMILTON

CONTENTS

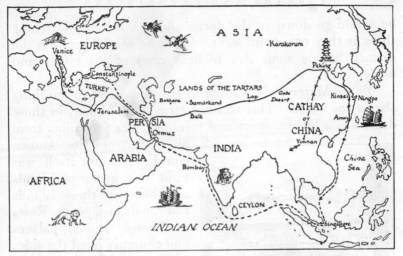

JOURNEYS OF MARCO POLO

I. THE ROAD TO CATHAY

Marco Polo

OVER six hundred years ago, two brothers, Nicolo and Maffeo Polo, sailed from the City of Venice. Their vessel took them to ports of the Eastern Mediterranean. There the two merchants planned to trade their goods and after making good bargains to return home with rich silks and jewels. Months passed; they did not return and their friends and relatives began to wonder what had happened to them; perhaps they had been murdered by robbers or had lost their lives at sea.

Nicolo, the elder brother, had left behind him a wife and a little son, Marco. As the years passed by and the boy grew a little older he often asked his mother about his father and his uncle. The poor woman sighed and, telling the story of their departure, said she feared that they were dead. Marco was sure that they were alive. Day after day

I

he would go down to the docks and spend hours watching ships as they came and went. Often he would question the seamen hoping some day to hear news of his father and uncle.

Young Marco Polo wanted to travel more than anything else in the world. This was not strange for Venice, in those days, was a busy seaport and meeting-place for sailors from

VENETIANS TRAVELLED ON THE CANALS IN GONDOLAS

all parts of the known world. The city itself was built on a group of islands and between these islands ran canals or lagoons. Rows of homes, stores, palaces and churches lined the sides of the canals and the Venetians travelled on the canals in gaily-coloured gondolas just as we travel on our streets in cars. The merchants of Venice sent ships out on the Mediterranean to trade in far-off ports and these ships brought back in their holds priceless cargoes of carpets, silks, spices and jewels. Many of these goods had come from the little-known countries of the East. They had been carried by camels over mountains and deserts for hundreds of miles. It was difficult for a boy brought up in such a city not to become interested in travel.

One morning when Marco was in his teens two foreign-looking men in tattered, travel-worn clothes stepped from a ship in the harbour of Venice and inquired for the Polo family. The men were Nicolo and Maffeo Polo. Nicolo's wife was dead, but when he met his son, a fine well-grown lad, his heart was cheered.

Marco Polo listened eagerly to the tales both men told of their long journey. He heard of their voyage to Constantinople and of how they had travelled overland, completed their business, and were ready to return home when they found that route was cut off by a tribe of savage men. They were forced to travel by another way and, in time, they came to the great trading city of Bokhara. There they stayed for three years. By chance, they fell in with a great nobleman who persuaded them to travel with him to the land of Cathay there to see for themselves the mighty Emperor Kublai Khan who, he assured them, would be greatly interested in seeing travellers from distant lands and would treat them well. On the way there, they were detained for many months by heavy storms, swollen rivers and steep mountain passes. It was another year before they arrived in Peking, the capital of Cathay.

Kublai Khan received them courteously and treated them like princes. He questioned them about the famous city of Venice for he knew much about western lands. When they had stayed for a time in Peking the Emperor requested them to return home with letters to the head of the Christian Church. They were also to get for him one hundred missionaries and some holy oil from the lamp in Christ's tomb in Jerusalem. A golden tablet or passport was given to them which stated that all rulers and chiefs in the Khan's kingdom were requested to treat these men well and give them safe conduct through their lands. Thus the journey home was made much easier.

These stirring stories thrilled young Marco Polo and he begged to be allowed to accompany his father and uncle when they returned to Cathay. Two years passed by; the Polos were trying to obtain missionaries to go with them

but in this they found great difficulty. Few men wanted
to face the dangers of such a long journey. In the end only
two missionaries were persuaded to accompany them. The
party of five set out by ship from Venice. It was twenty-
five years before they were to see their city again.

THEY HAD TO CROSS THE GOBI DESERT

First they made their way to Jerusalem where the holy
oil was obtained. From Jerusalem they travelled overland.
The way was full of hardships and dangers. In a short time,
the two missionaries lost heart and would go no farther.
The party of three continued on its way. Many months
later they reached the city of Ormuz which was famous for
its trade in spices, pearls, gold and precious stones. There
they joined a caravan of great two-humped camels which
set out in a north-easterly direction for the cities of Kashgar and Balk. During the journey Marco Polo observed
and made notes about all the wonders he saw, the long

caravans, the strange people, the animals, the trees. He wrote about all of them with enthusiasm. But the long journey over the hot plains and deserts was too much for the lad. He fell ill with fever and because of this misfortune the travellers were delayed for a year while he rested and regained his strength.

The greatest hardship of all now faced the Polos for they had to cross the Gobi Desert, where even today neither bird nor beast is to be found. Travellers are warned when crossing it to provide food for themselves for a month. Stories were told of men who, having lost their way and in danger of starving, were forced to kill their donkeys and camels for food. Men in these desolate regions, it was said, heard horrible voices and evil spirits which lured them away from the caravan to their deaths. Travellers on the desert were warned to keep close together. Bells were hung on the camels' necks so that they could be found should they stray away from the others. For over thirty days the Polos journeyed eastward, travelling between the few wells of water that were to be found, before they arrived in the land of Cathay where they were met by messengers of the Great Khan.

Following the line of the Great Wall of China they reached and crossed a hump-backed bridge of pure marble which has ever since been known as *The Bridge of Marco Polo*. In May, 1275, the Polos reached the city of Peking after a journey which had taken close to four years.

They were brought before the Emperor who was seated on a splendid throne glittering with gold and diamonds. He bade them welcome and thanked them for the holy oil. After hearing the story of their journey he asked who the handsome young lad with them was and Nicolo replied, "This is your servant and my son." "He is welcome," said the Khan. "Because he pleases me much I shall give him a place among my officers." A great feast was given in their honour, and the Polos were invited to live at the palace.

Marco Polo soon learned the customs of Cathay. He put aside his Italian clothes for the long silken robes of the Chinese. So clever was he in learning, that in a remarkably short time he could speak and write the four languages used in Cathay. As he grew older, the Khan, who had a great liking for this intelligent young man, entrusted him with difficult tasks and sent him on missions to distant parts of his kingdom. Marco Polo observed everything he saw and put down in his notes accounts of strange and amusing things which he thought might interest the Emperor. So greatly did he please Kublai Khan that honours and riches were heaped on him. He was even made governor of an important town for a three year period.

Marco Polo visited places where no Europeans had ever been before, Burma, Tibet, the island of Java, and he even travelled by sea to India. He wrote in his diary that in many ways the Chinese were far ahead of the Europeans of his time. Coal was used by the Chinese over seven hundred years ago. This coal, he wrote, was dug from the mountains and used for fuel and was found to be more lasting than wood for it kept the houses warm all through the night and burned till morning. Chinese people he found to be very clean. Every man of wealth in the city of Kinsai in South China had a marble bath in his home and in that city alone, there were three thousand baths. The Chinese had learned how to use oil as fuel in lamps and men came from distant parts of Cathay to the oil wells to procure the precious liquid. He wrote about the mineral, asbestos, which was obtained from the rocks, woven into cloth and used by the Chinese because of its fireproof qualities. In China the art of printing had been practised for many years and Chinese printed their own books while Europeans were still struggling along copying books by hand. Printed paper money was in use and it was found to be much lighter and easier to carry about than heavy gold and silver coins. Marco Polo spoke also of the making of silk and of fine porcelain.

Marco Polo spent much time with Kublai Khan in the royal palace and greatly admired the King of Kings. He described him as "a man of middle stature, that is, neither tall nor short; his complexion is fair, his eyes are black and

KUBLAI KHAN WAS SEATED ON A SPLENDID THRONE

handsome, his nose well-shaped and prominent." His palace was built of marble and contained fine sculptures, tapestries and paintings of dragons, animals and flowers. The roofs of the many buildings in the grounds were tiled in bright colours—green, red, blue and violet. A high wall surrounded the buildings and gardens and the distance around the royal grounds was so great that it took a horseman all day to make the journey. A strange sight that was seen daily was that of a large lion which moved about, unchained, through the palace gardens. When it was led into the presence of the Khan it was trained to drop to its knees and bow, humbling itself before this mighty monarch.

The many feasts which the Emperor gave were famous for their magnificence and grandeur. At the dinners, the Khan sat on a throne which was higher than those of his officers and guests; even his royal sons sat with their heads on the same level as his feet. Dozens of servants waited on him, their faces covered with veils so that their breath might not harm his food. A page brought his winecup to him and as the cup was put to his lips musicians played. On such occasions guests from distant parts of the Empire brought gifts of great value to their ruler. At one time he received five thousand camels, five thousand elephants and one hundred thousand horses. He was continually receiving great quantities of spices from India, pearls from Persia, rubies from Ceylon and jade from distant parts of China.

But the greatest marvel of his kingdom was the capital city of Peking, which Kublai Khan had rebuilt in the form of a square. Here Kublai Khan held his court each year from December to February. The wall around the city was twenty-four miles long and it contained twelve fine gates, each of which was defended by one thousand guards. The streets were broad and so straight that a guard above a gate on the northern wall could clearly see one standing on the gate of the southern wall six miles away. Each evening at sundown a bell in a tall tower in the midst of the city rang three times to tell everyone that the city gates were closed until morning.

In spite of all this grandeur, as the years passed by, the Polos longed to return to their native city, Venice, once more. The Khan, however, was unwilling to allow them to leave, for in the seventeen years that they had spent in Cathay the Emperor had grown to depend on them, especially on Marco Polo. He charged them with being ungrateful and promised Marco Polo greater riches and more power if he would only promise to stay. "Have I not done everything possible for you?" he asked. Their chance to return home came in a strange way.

At that time a beautiful Chinese princess, Kogatin, was to be married to the King of Persia. At first Kublai Khan planned to send her to the Persian court by the overland route, but he had to abandon that idea for he feared that she would be wearied by the long journey over the Gobi Desert or that she might be killed by fierce tribesmen in the dangerous mountain passes of Persia. Marco Polo, who had just returned from a trip to

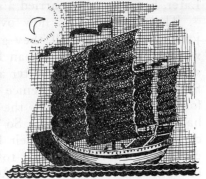

GREAT SHIPS WERE FITTED FOR THE JOURNEY

India, by sea, suggested that she might travel by ship from Cathay to her new home. He proposed that he himself should lead the expedition. With a heavy heart, the Khan at last gave his consent to this plan.

Fourteen great ships each manned by two hundred and fifty men were fitted out for the journey. Rich presents of jewels were given to the Polos as farewell gifts and golden passports were again presented to them. After farewells were made the fleet sailed through the China Sea, passed the Spice Islands and arrived at the island of Sumatra. Here they were forced to wait for five months till furious storms at sea were over and fair weather had come. Marco Polo describes the island of Ceylon on the south-eastern coast of India as "the finest island in the world". After eighteen months the fleet reached the port of Ormuz, on the Gulf of Persia. The trip had been so long and trying that two Persian ambassadors, twenty of the royal attendants and six hundred of the crew had died on the way. Bad news awaited Princess Kogatin. The King of Persia, whom she was to have married, had died many months before. Later, however, she married a son of the King.

Their mission was now over. From Persia the Polos journeyed overland till they gazed once more on the blue waters of the Mediterranean Sea. There they boarded a ship and reached Venice after an absence of nearly twenty-five years. No one in Venice believed that these bearded foreign-looking men were the Polos; even their relatives had believed them dead. So the travellers thought of a clever way to convince their friends and relatives. They planned a magnificent feast to which they invited all their relatives and former friends. As each course was served, the Polos entered the room in different rich clothes, first, robes of crimson satin, next, crimson damask and finally crimson velvet. After the last course the Polos left the room and re-entered carrying in their arms the tattered travel-stained clothes which they had worn when they arrived in the city. With a sharp knife Marco Polo slashed the clothes here and there and from the seams there poured forth jewels of great value, rubies, sapphires, diamonds and emeralds. The guests were filled with wonder at the great show of wealth. They were at last convinced that these strangers were, in truth, Nicolo, Maffeo and Marco Polo.

A few years later war broke out between Genoa and Venice. Marco Polo was captured by the Genoese and remained for three years in prison. While there he told the story of his travels to a fellow-prisoner who, greatly interested, persuaded Marco Polo to dictate to him the story of his journey through Asia and his life in Cathay. When

Marco Polo was freed he returned to Venice, where he lived quietly for the rest of his life.

Marco Polo was the greatest traveller of his time. The book of his travels opened the eyes of the people of Europe to the wonders of the East and inspired others to find out more about the world.

TEST

Choose the word or words that will make the statement true.

1. Cathay is now called   (1) China
                           (2) Ceylon
                           (3) Japan

2. Marco Polo, one of the first Europeans to visit Cathay, was born in   (1) Cairo
                (2) Venice
                (3) Genoa

3. In order to reach Cathay, Marco Polo had to cross the
                           (1) Sahara Desert
                           (2) Gobi Desert
                           (3) Kalahari Desert

4. He travelled most of the way to Cathay using (1) horses
                                       (2) oxen
                                       (3) camels

5. One of the important cities he visited on the journey was
                           (1) Genoa
                           (2) Calicut
                           (3) Balk

6. When he arrived in Cathay he was received by the mighty ruler (1) Kublai Khan
            (2) Aga Khan
            (3) Genghis Khan

7. Marco Polo was amazed to find that the people of Kinsai, a city in Cathay, took a bath (1) once in a lifetime
                                (2) once a year
                              (3) many times a year

8. Marco Polo spent (1) two years in Cathay
                     (2) five years in Cathay
                     (3) seventeen years in Cathay

9. Some of the riches Marco Polo brought back from Cathay
   were (1) furs
         (2) jewels
         (3) amber

10. After Marco Polo came home from his journey to Cathay,
    merchants from Europe   (1) journeyed to Cathay to trade
                            (2) took little interest in trade
                                with Cathay.

THINGS TO DO TOGETHER

1. Put a large map of Europe and Asia on the side blackboard in
   chalk. Trace the route taken by Marco Polo on his return
   home from Cathay. Locate the following places on the map:
   Ormuz, Ceylon, Sumatra, Venice, Peking.

2. On a large strip of paper draw a series of pictures which tell
   the story of Marco Polo's journey from Venice to Peking.
   Some suggestions for the illustrations are: (1) Saying farewell to friends in Venice (2) Crossing the Gobi Desert
   (3) Crossing over the Marco Polo Bridge in Cathay (4) Being
   presented to the Emperor of Cathay.

3. Act some of the scenes described in this story. Choose the
   ones you like best. Talk over what you would like to do and
   say. Choose those in the class who would be suited for these
   parts and try out your ideas. Here are some suggestions:
   (1) Marco Polo telling the Emperor of Cathay about the
   strange things he saw in Cathay (2) The great feast given by
   the Polos when they returned home.

4. Collect all the Chinese articles that you can find. Some of
   these things will probably be (1) Chop-sticks (2) Shoes for
   bound feet (3) Chinese money.

THINGS TO DO SEPARATELY

1. What is the meaning of each of the following words? If you do not know look these words up in your dictionary.
   asbestos, porcelain, caravans, gondola, Chinese junk.
2. Make a collection of pictures of China. Include in your group, pictures of pagodas, Chinese junks, Chinese temples, Chinese coolies.

BOOKS TO READ

FOR THE TEACHER

Great Navigators and Discoverers. J. A. Brendon. *Geo. G. Harrap & Co.*

Exploration and Discovery, Arthur Archer. *Cambridge University Press.*

A History of Geographical Discovery and Exploration, J. N. L. Baker. *Geo. G. Harrap & Co. Ltd.*

FOR THE PUPIL

Boys' Book of Exploration, J. Harris Gable. *E. P. Dutton & Co.*

A Book of Discovery, M. B. Synge. *Thos. Nelson & Sons.*

They Went Exploring, Arensa Sondergaard. *Harper & Bros.*

Map Makers, Cottler and Jaffe. *The Ryerson Press.*

They Put Out to Sea, Roger Duvoisin. *Alfred A. Knopf.*

Heroes of Discovery, Robert Finch. *University of London Press.*

THE CARAVAN ROUTE TO THE EAST

For many years after the time of Marco Polo, merchants from Genoa and Venice followed the overland route taken by the Polos to the East. After the sea voyage through the Mediterranean Sea to cities located on the eastern shores of the great sea, the travellers journeyed to Ormuz, a city of great wealth and immense trade on the Gulf of Persia. Many of the traders went no further east but bought spices, precious stones, pearls, and silks and returned home to sell their riches at fine profits.

Others who were more daring ventured along the caravan route to the famous trading city of Balk which was midway between the east and the west. Some went a little further east to the cities of Kashgar, Yarkand, and Khotan. It was the hope of greater gain that took these men so far from home for they knew that in these distant places they could buy their merchandise at much lower prices and thus line their pockets with more gold.

The most daring of all the traders journeyed east over plains and through mountain passes till they reached the city of Lob on the border of the Gobi Desert. The crossing of the desert was full of dangers and could only be made under the leadership of experienced guides. It took well over a month to cross the dreary wasteland of hills and valleys of sand. Not a thing could be found to eat and there were only a few wells of fresh water. The guides charged fabulous sums of money to take caravans safely across the desert and on to the heart of Cathay.

To the north of the main caravan route lay the two great cities of Samarkand and Kara Korum which were also important trading centres. Samarkand was a city of immense wealth and for that reason men in those days spoke of the Golden Road to Samarkand; but for many a traveller the road was far from being a golden one. The journey there led over deserts and through mountainous regions which were infested by robbers. Along the sides of the road lay the bleached bones of many an unlucky trader who had been attacked and killed by these fierce thieves.

For more than a hundred years after the death of Marco Polo these caravan routes were used by scores of European traders. The great Khans of Cathay had soldiers posted along the trading routes to guard travellers from harm. The roads themselves were kept in good condition and inns were located every few miles along the highways. In these inns travellers could obtain food and shelter.

However, when the powerful empire of Cathay began to crumble, the caravan routes were no longer safe to travel. The Khan's soldiers were sorely needed at home to defend Cathay itself and had been withdrawn. Fierce robbers plundered any caravans which dared to venture along the roads. The Turks overran all the lands to the east of the Mediterranean Sea and demanded huge taxes from Europeans travelling through their lands. Merchants from Genoa and Venice dared not travel by the overland route and began to search for some other way to the East.

TEST

Which statements are true and which are false?
1. Travellers from Venice and Genoa journeyed east to buy spices and jewels.
2. In Marco Polo's time, the caravan route to the East was well guarded by soldiers of the Great Khan of Cathay.
3. The great trading city of Ormuz was at the eastern end of the Mediterranean Sea.
4. The famous city of Lob was on the border of the Gobi Desert.

5. Experienced guides took caravans across the Gobi Desert in less than twelve days.
6. Inns where travellers could rest were located every few miles along the highway.
7. The largest city on the main caravan route was Samarkand.
8. After Marco Polo's death, the caravan routes continued to be used for three hundred years.
9. When the empire of Cathay began to crumble, the caravan routes became infested by robbers.
10. When the routes became unsafe, merchants from Venice and Genoa gave up their desire to trade with the East.

THINGS TO DO TOGETHER

1. Make a large class mural showing a caravan travelling over the desert.
2. On a large blackboard map of Europe and Asia mark in the main caravan route. On it locate the following places: Gobi Desert, Peking, Lob, Ormuz and Balk. Mark in also Samarkand and Kara Korum.
3. Discuss why camels are used in the desert regions instead of horses.

THINGS TO DO SEPARATELY

1. Collect specimens of spices; put them in cellophane envelopes; label and mount them on a large piece of cardboard. Print this title at the top of your poster *Spices from the East*. Find out where each spice is grown and one use for each spice.
2. Cut out pictures of jewels from booklets printed for jewelry firms. Try to obtain coloured pictures of the following jewels: emeralds, sapphires, amethysts, pearls, rubies, and diamonds.
3. Find out why people in Marco Polo's time were willing to pay fabulous sums for spices.

Solving the Riddle of Distant Africa

Prince Henry, the Navigator

When the Turks barred Europeans from travelling over the old caravan routes to India and China, men began to wonder if it was possible to go to the East by another route. Arab traders still sold pepper, ginger, cinnamon, silks, jewels and perfumes but Europeans knew that they were being charged far too much for these precious things. Seamen who had sailed along the coast of Africa returned saying that ships might be able to reach India by a sea-route by sailing down the coast of Africa, if that coast, at last, curved to the east.

One of the first men to become interested in this scheme to reach India was Henry, third son of the King of Portugal. Because his land faced the sea, he and his countrymen had always been interested in the ocean and ships, and many Portuguese earned their living by the sea. When only a small boy, Prince Henry had watched the vessels come into the harbour from far-off lands and he had questioned the sailors about the strange places that they had visited.

When Prince Henry became a man, his interest in ships and sailors grew. It seemed to him that ships which were to go on long dangerous voyages needed to be more seaworthy than the ones used at that time. Sailors, he thought, did not know enough about their sails, ships, supplies, maps and some of the instruments of navigation. Prince Henry decided to start a school for seamen on a rocky point of land jutting out into the Atlantic Ocean, known as Cape St. Vincent. Here the prince studied and taught others all he knew. He felt that he could be of more help to his people by remaining at home and taking care of the ships and supplies than by going to sea himself. Sailors came to his naval school and after a thorough training were sent out as skilled mariners. At St. Vincent, they learned about new instruments of navigation, the astrolabe, which told the sailors exactly where they were on the map, and the mariner's compass whose little needle, always pointing to the north, guided men when they could not see the sun, moon or stars in cloudy times. Here at his palace, men lived, worked and learned all that Prince Henry could teach them about the sea.

Each year several ships were sent by him down the coast of Africa and when they returned they reported about the coast-line, the winds and tides, the people and the climate. All of these facts were recorded in log-books which the captains were instructed to keep. At each new place they visited, a tower was built which acted as a landmark to ships passing along the coast.

Prince Henry had to teach seamen that many things they believed were untrue. Some mariners believed that if they were to sail very far to the south they would get nearer and nearer to the sun, that their skin would become black and that they would at last be burned to cinders. Another story was that there were fire-breathing monsters ready to swallow up the ships and crews which ventured far from the shore of Africa. Because of these terrifying things, ships never travelled far from land and, at night, anchored in a bay or harbour till dawn. Still another story was that the continent of Africa stretched on and on to the south forever and that no ship could sail around it to the east. The Prince, through long years of teaching, succeeded partly in showing seamen that many of their ideas were false and their fears groundless. Some did not believe him. "Why does he choose to shut himself up in his tower and waste his time studying?" they asked. "Why does he send seamen along the African coast trying to find a route to

India and China? This can never be done. Prince Henry is quite mad even to think of these things." Paying no heed to the unbelievers, Henry continued to study, to learn all he could and to encourage others to carry out his plans.

Most of the sailing ships of those days had one great awkward square sail but at Prince Henry's school, new types of sails were planned, triangular in shape, with the wide side at the bottom and the sharp tip at the top of the mast. These new ships, safer and easier to handle, were known as caravels and proved of great use when sudden storms blew up off the rocky coast of Africa.

Two seamen who volunteered to sail down the coast of Africa were, by chance, blown out to sea by a gale and lost sight of the coast. Next morning when the storm had spent itself they found, to their surprise, an island not far away to the west. They hastened to land. Because they were so overjoyed at escaping from death at sea, they named this island Porto Santo which means Holy Port. When they returned to Portugal, they told Prince Henry of their discovery and he sent out colonists to live on the island. Among other things, the colonists took with them a pair of rabbits which were turned loose. Unfortunately there were no enemies of the rabbits on the island and in less than three years there were so many rabbits that they ate up all the green things growing there and the settlement had to be given up. However the settlers did not have to return home. Something that looked like land had been observed to the west. Sailing to it, the settlers came to a beautiful island with graceful palm trees waving in the breeze. Here they settled, and to it they gave the name Madeira. Madeira still belongs to Portugal. It is famous for the fine needlework done on linen cloths by the skilful women who live there.

A seaman, more daring than the others, rounded Cape

Bojador which was called Jutting-out Cape, and returned joyfully, reporting that he had found no sea-serpents, no sheets of flame, no boiling waters there, but an ocean as easy to sail upon as the waters at home. Sailors began to lose some of the fears that had held them back, and year after year they explored further and further along the coast. They discovered a great white cape which they named Cape Blanco and there they found Arabs who traded with the Portuguese. In the holds of their ships they brought back brass, silver and gold and also helpless negroes, captured by the Arabs and sold as slaves. Thus began the slave trade in Africa. Seamen grew rich in this new trade and Prince Henry no longer had to urge men to go forth on these voyages. From towns on the banks of the Senegal and Gambia rivers, Portuguese sea-captains returned home with great quantities of gold and silver. Further to the south, a lovely little group of islands was discovered, and because the leaves on the plants and trees there were so fresh and green, they were named the Cape Verde Islands.

In all, two thousand miles of coast was charted by the Portuguese sailors and on a great wall map, six feet in height, Prince Henry drew in the coast-line and marked all the places his seamen had visited. The Prince himself never went on any of these long trips, but he inspired others to do great things. As the years passed by his country's ships and seamen became famous and were, before long, known as the best in all Europe. This was all due to Prince Henry the Navigator.

After teaching for forty years at his naval school at St. Vincent, Prince Henry died. He did not live to see fulfilled his plan of reaching India by sea, but the work was continued by others who remembered their beloved Prince Henry to whom they owed so much. Even the smallest school boy in Portugal to-day can tell without hesitating of the life and work of this famous man who did so much to make the Portuguese a race of seamen and traders.

TEST
Answer the following questions in sentences:
1. Prince Henry's father was ruler of what country?
2. What was Prince Henry's plan for finding a way to the East?
3. Where was Prince Henry's naval school located?
4. Why were his sailors afraid to sail far out from the coast?
5. Prince Henry's sailors studied about two instruments of navigation at the naval school. Name the two instruments.
6. What three islands did the sailors discover?
7. Name two capes reached by Prince Henry's sailors.
8. By what title is Prince Henry known?

THINGS TO DO TOGETHER
1. You are a sailor of the time of Prince Henry and your ship is sailing down the coast of Africa. What are some of the dangers you are afraid of if you go far away from the coast?
2. On a map of Africa, locate the places mentioned in the story.

THINGS TO DO SEPARATELY
1. Try to get a mariner's compass and see how it works.
2. Find out one product that Portugal sends to Canada.
3. What do the women on the island of Madeira send to Canada?

BARTHOLOMEW DIAZ

Bartholomew Diaz, a skilful Portuguese sailor, carried on the work so ably begun by Prince Henry the Navigator. To him the King of Portugal gave three caravels with instructions to sail down the coast of Africa, to find, if possible, the southern tip of the continent and to continue on till he should reach India.

From Portugal, Diaz sailed further and further south along the coast of Africa till he found that the sun at noon was directly over his head and that the heat from it was almost unbearable. Some days later, he found that the sun at noon was to the north of his ships. This surprised him greatly. Without knowing it, Diaz had crossed the Equator and was in the South Atlantic. He steered his ships southward along a coast never before reached by white men. His sailors grew curious to find out what kind of land this was along which they were sailing. Orders were given to lower the boats and put to shore. The landing place was named Diaz Point after the commander and there a pillar was erected on which was his name and that of King John of Portugal. This pillar remained for hundreds of years as a landmark to sailors and the ruins of it may be seen even to-day. The sailors gazed in wonder at herds of strange-looking animals with long necks; these were giraffes.

On his way south, Diaz had stayed close to the coast, but now a severe storm arose and drove his ships far out to sea. For two weeks the gale blew, tearing the sails into shreds and filling the sailors with terror. The weather became colder and colder and the waves rougher and wilder till the tired and weary sailors looked only for shipwreck and death. When at last the seas grew calm, Diaz ordered his vessels on a course to the north-east. In a few days the little fleet came within sight of land. Although Diaz did not know it, he had rounded the southern tip of Africa and was well over a hundred miles up the eastern coast.

Food was growing scarce and the fresh-water casks were empty. Orders were given to land. On a hillside, Diaz saw natives tending sheep and cows, so he named the inlet Cowherd's Bay. To-day it is called Algoa Bay. The Portuguese tried to make friends with the black men who tended the sheep but the frightened natives fled inland. Never before had they seen such strange men with pale faces nor such ships as these caravels with their great sails.

When Diaz told his crew of his plans to go on up the coast to India the men were not pleased. Many were ill. They pleaded with Diaz to turn back. Diaz had high hopes of reaching India but he could only persuade his men to sail along the coast for three more days. At the mouth of the Great Fish River, Diaz landed and put up another pillar, the last one he erected. The commander again begged his men to go on but they refused to listen to him. Diaz gazed out across the sea towards what he felt sure was India, then with a heavy heart he turned his ships back on their homeward way.

On the way back, Diaz kept close to the shore and after a few days he sighted a great headland. Because a great storm was raging as he passed this towering mass of rock, he named it the Cape of Storms. Beyond this cape, the land turned sharply to the north. Diaz realized that he had passed the southern tip of Africa, the place that Prince Henry's sailors had tried to find for over forty years.

When Diaz reported to him on his voyage, King John was overjoyed with the news that Diaz brought. "But," said the King, "let us not call the southern tip of this land the Cape of Storms, for if we do, men will be afraid to pass it. Let us name it the Cape of Good Hope for it fills our hearts with joy and hope. We are now certain to find a sea-route to India before long."

TEST

Complete the story below by inserting appropriate words in the blank spaces:

Bartholomew Diaz tried to find a sea-route to ———— by sailing around the continent of ————. Sailing south through the ———— Ocean he was driven by storms far out to sea. Without knowing it, Diaz had rounded the southern tip of

————————. The ships made their way to land where they took on supplies of food and fresh ————————. To this place Diaz gave the name Cowherd's Bay; to-day it is called ———————— Bay. When the sailors reached ———————— River they refused to go any further. Diaz reached home again and he told his king that he had named the southern tip of Africa the Cape of ———————— but the king changed its name to the Cape of ————————.

THINGS TO DO TOGETHER

1. On a map of Africa locate the following places: Madeira, Cape Blanco, Cape of Good Hope, Algoa Bay, Great Fish River. Mark in with dotted lines the route taken by Diaz.
2. Act the scene in the story where Diaz returned to the King of Portugal and told him of his journey. Do not forget the part in which he tells the king of the Cape of Storms. It is better to try out speeches rather than to write out the words.

THINGS TO DO SEPARATELY

1. Find pictures of (1) animals of South Africa (2) trees (3) natives (4) natives' homes (5) Cape of Good Hope.
2. On a map of Africa, locate at least five cities in South Africa.

Vasco da Gama

For nearly seventy years Portuguese sailors had been trying to find a sea-route to India. Now Vasco da Gama, who was high in favour with King Manuel, was given command of four ships and told to search for the route that Prince Henry the Navigator and Bartholomew Diaz had both tried to find. Vasco da Gama had already proved himself to be a skilful sailor; he was also a good leader of men.

On a hot July morning in 1497, his ships rode at anchor in the harbour of Saigres. At sunrise he had gone to the church built by Prince Henry the Navigator and asked God to bless his voyage and guide him safely to India. A long procession of priests, monks and merchants accompanied da Gama down to the docks. Many of them feared that they might never see him again. Amidst tears, cheers and fond farewells, the little vessels pulled up anchor and before long vanished from sight.

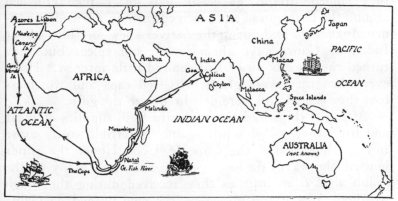

THE SEA-ROUTE TO INDIA

At the Canary and Cape Verde Islands, supplies of fruit, meat and fresh water were taken on board. Here Diaz, who had accompanied him thus far and had given da Gama much help and advice, bade his friend farewell and returned to Portugal. With a blue sky above and a fair wind driving them on, the ships headed in a southerly direction. Da Gama decided not to stay as close to the shore of Africa as the other explorers had done for he feared the dangers of hidden rocks and unknown coasts. His plan was to strike out in a south-westerly direction into an unknown part of the Atlantic. In doing this, he hoped to make the journey to the Cape of Good Hope in a shorter time.

As day after day passed by, the only things the sailors saw were great sea-turtles, monster sharks and schools of flying fish. For ninety-six days, the vessels travelled on without sight of land. Food began to go bad, water became foul-smelling and the sailors grew sickly and weak. It was only by good leadership that da Gama was able to persuade the crew to continue. The first land sighted was a little inlet which the Portuguese named St. Helena Bay. Here they landed. Bands of small ugly black men crowded around the Portuguese and received them in a friendly manner. Anxious to find out if the natives knew anything about India, da Gama gave them jewels and spices but they turned their heads away and showed little interest. However when they were given bells, red caps and worthless toys they smiled and were delighted with the gifts.

After the ships had taken aboard fresh supplies of meat and fruit, they sailed south again. A terrible storm arose just as they neared the Cape of Good Hope; the winds howled, the waves dashed over the ships and many of the sailors died from injuries they received during the rough weather. Weary and homesick, the men begged da Gama to turn back but he vowed he would throw the first man into the sea who in future even so much as whispered of turning back. When the seas grew calm, da Gama realized that he had sailed around the dreaded Cape of Good Hope. With joyful hearts, he and his men thanked God for their deliverance. Soon the ships arrived at the little bay discovered by Diaz and named Cowherd's Bay. One of the ships was so badly damaged that it had to be left behind. The others went on. One by one, the crosses, erected by Diaz to guide ships, were passed and the little fleet headed into unknown waters.

On December 25, they named a coast which they were passing Natal in memory of Jesus' birthday or natal day. When they landed further along the coast, they made

friends with a tribe of tall negroes known as Bantus who
lived in very clean huts, shaped like beehives. These tribesmen were brave, fierce hunters and brought da Gama
antelope, giraffes and lions which they had killed with their
spears, long bows and arrows. The Portuguese gladly
accepted an invitation to sleep in their huts but the natives
kept peering with wonder at the visitors with their strange,
white faces and odd, black
beards. Vasco da Gama and
his men got little sleep.

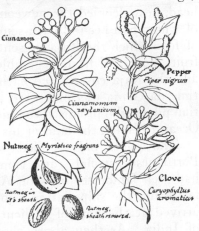

SPICES FROM THE EAST

Returning to the ships,
da Gama again set sail. One
morning a low-lying coral
island was sighted. This was
the island of Mozambique.
In the harbour, the Portuguese saw four ocean-going
vessels riding at anchor.
These fine ships were owned
by Arabs and were laden
with pepper, ginger, cinnamon, nutmeg, precious stones
and silk. The Arabs had brought them from India. Vasco
da Gama's heart beat quickly as he questioned the traders
about India. They told him that in India precious stones
were so plentiful that they had to be gathered in baskets.
The Arabs only laughed at the poor gifts that da Gama
offered them and asked for scarlet silks and gold. Anger
plainly showed in the Arabs' faces when they learned that
the Portuguese were Christians. The Arabs planned to do
the Portuguese harm but da Gama and his sailors were able
to escape. Later at Mombassa, the Portuguese were welcomed at first by the Arabs, but when the latter learned

that these men were Christians they, too, turned on them. Luckily da Gama made his escape under cover of darkness just before a planned attack took place.

A much more friendly welcome awaited the explorer at the seaport of Melinda. The Raja or ruler came out in a great canoe. Under a crimson umbrella, dressed in a gorgeous satin robe and with a richly embroidered turban on his head, he welcomed the newcomers. The Portuguese, many of whom had been ill with scurvy, were delighted with gifts of food which the Raja presented to them, three fine sheep, fruit, meat and fresh vegetables. For nine days da Gama and the Raja entertained each other. At the end of that time da Gama was presented by the Raja with two Christian pilots who promised to guide his ships across the Indian Ocean to India, the land of his dreams.

The pilots only smiled when they were shown the Portuguese astrolabe and compass for they declared they had seen far better ones on Arabs' ships. Favoured by a fair wind, the ships, after a journey of twenty-three days, arrived at the port of Calicut on the south-western coast of India. As they approached the shore, the Portuguese gazed in wonder at the tall towers and beautiful white palaces of the city.

Vasco da Gama wanted to make a good impression on the Indians so he and twelve of his officers went ashore dressed in full armour with banners waving and trumpets blowing. On a golden litter carried by four black slaves, da Gama was taken through the streets to the royal palace of the Zamorin or ruler. Crowds of curious Indians all along the route gazed at him in wonder from the streets, the trees and roof-tops. In a court-yard of his palace, the Zamorin, seated on a throne of silver and gold cloth, received da Gama. The Zamorin was richly dressed and wore a great crown of gold and jewels on his head. Vasco da Gama told him of Portugal and of King Manuel who was lord of many lands. He said that he had come on this long and dangerous journey to trade and bring back gems, spices and silks to Portugal. That night, at the Zamorin's invitation, da Gama slept in one of the luxurious apartments in the royal palace.

When the jealous Arabs in Calicut learned of da Gama's good fortune they set to work to stir up trouble. They not only hated the Portuguese because he was a Christian, but also because he had come to start up trade with India. They told false stories to the Zamorin and said that da Gama had come to rob the city of its riches. They even plotted to seize and destroy the Portuguese ships in the harbour. In spite of these rumours and plots, da Gama traded and soon his ships

THE ZAMORIN WAS RICHLY DRESSED

were loaded with spices from India, silks from China, jewels from Ceylon and fine rugs from Persia. An Indian idol of gold with emerald eyes as big as walnuts was carefully stowed away in the hold. This was a gift from the Zamorin to His Majesty, King Manuel of Portugal.

With their ships weighed down with treasures, the Portuguese set sail for home. Before they had gone far the wind dropped and the ships were unable to go on. It was on that very day that the Arabs had planned to attack da Gama's ships. The Arab ships, with angry armed men aboard, approached the Portuguese bent on butchering them. Nearer and nearer they came brandishing their weapons and thirsting to torture and kill. At that moment a sudden gust of wind blew and filled the sails of the Portuguese ships carrying them out to sea and leaving the bloodthirsty Arabs far behind. By this strange piece of luck, the Portuguese fleet was saved from disaster.

The journey to India had taken eleven months; the return journey took one year, for storms at sea and sickness among the crew delayed the return. Of the one hundred and seventy men who had set out only fifty-five returned. Many had died of scurvy, a disease that is caused by a lack of fresh fruits and vegetables in the diet.

Crowds flocked down to the harbour as Vasco da Gama and his men stepped ashore. The news of his great success travelled quickly to the royal palace where he was summoned for an audience with King Manuel. When da Gama told his thrilling story and showed the riches he had brought back, King Manuel's joy knew no bounds. He heaped high honours on the brave captain, made him a knight, gave him a pension of 3000 ducats a year and named him Admiral of the Indies. Amidst all of this excitement, Vasco da Gama did not forget to go to the little chapel of Prince Henry where he had prayed before he had set out, and give thanks to God for the success of his voyage and for his safe return.

A sea-route to India had been found. Vasco da Gama had opened up a route which was to be used by traders for over four hundred years. In a few years the city of Calicut became a Portuguese trading station and Arab traders had now good reason to be jealous of the trade Portugal carried on with the East.

Vasco da Gama had made the dreams of Prince Henry, the Navigator come true.

TEST

Tell which word or words in Column II matches another group of words in Column I.

COLUMN I	COLUMN II
1. Vasco da Gama's homeland.	a—Natal
2. Vasco da Gama's plan.	b—spices, silks, jewels, rugs
3. Place he passed on Christmas Day.	c—Melinda
4. Place in Africa where he received two pilots.	d—scurvy
5. The city da Gama reached in India.	e—Admiral of the Indies
6. Disease from which many of his men suffered.	f—Portugal
7. The riches da Gama brought back from India.	g—Calicut
8. Title given to da Gama by King Manuel.	h—sea-route to India

THINGS TO DO TOGETHER

1. On a map trace the route showing Vasco da Gama's voyage from Portugal to India. On your map locate the following places: Melinda, Calicut, Cape of Good Hope, Natal, Atlantic Ocean, Portugal, Indian Ocean.

2. Make a sketch showing Vasco da Gama being presented to the Zamorin in his royal palace in Calicut.

THINGS TO DO SEPARATELY

1. Imagine that you are taking a sea voyage from Canada to India. Through what waters would you pass on your journey (1) if you sailed from Halifax, (2) if you sailed from Vancouver?

2. Find a picture of the famous building in India, the Taj Mahal.

BOOKS TO READ

For the Teacher

Great Navigators and Discoverers, J. A. Brendon. *George G. Harrap & Co. Ltd.*

Stories of Exploration and Discovery, Arthur Archer. *Cambridge University Press.*

Unrolling the Map, Leonard Outhwaite. *McClelland & Stewart Ltd.*

Book of Discovery, M. B. Synge. *Thos. Nelson & Sons Limited.*

He Went With Vasco da Gama, L. A. Kent. *Houghton Mifflin & Co.*

Heroes of Discovery, R. J. Finch. *University of London Press.*

They Put Out to Sea, R. A. Duvoisin. *Alfred A. Knopf, Inc.*

For the Pupil

The Book of Discovery, T. C. Bridges. *George G. Harrap & Co. Ltd.*

They Went Exploring, Arensa Sondergaard. *Harper & Bros.*

THE NORSEMEN LAND IN NORTH AMERICA.

II. DISCOVERING THE NEW WORLD
The Norse Sea Rovers

HUNDREDS of years ago in North-western Europe, there lived a race of fearless and sturdy men who were known as Vikings or Norsemen. These fair-haired, blue-eyed people had been driven to the sea to make a living because of the mountainous nature of their country and the lack of suitable farmland. From the deep bays (called wiks or fiords) along the coast of Scandinavia, they ventured forth into stormy seas to fish, to trade and often to plunder ships at sea, and settlements on shore.

In time, the more daring of the Vikings crossed to the islands that reach out into the Atlantic like stepping stones, the Orkneys, Shetlands, Faroes and even far-off Iceland.

Their sleek, swift long-ships were built of oak and caulked with cow's hair spun into a cord. On the prow was a carved figure, often the grinning face and head of a fierce golden dragon. Along the sides of the ship were slung rows of finely polished shields. The single square sail, bright with coloured stripes, carried the ship over the waves like a great bird. Viking ships were of two types. The smaller ones were used for the shorter, less dangerous journeys along the coast. They had sixteen pairs of oars. The larger vessels had thirty-two pairs of oars. These were used for the long voyages out into the stormy ocean. Norse ships were, for hundreds of years, unequalled by those of any other people.

Norsemen were proud and independent in nature. When in the year 872, Harold the Fair-haired, came to rule over Norway, he made a law that no man could own private property but must rent the land from the King. Many Vikings who could not bear to live under a tyrant left their homes in Norway and settled in far-away Iceland. This small colony grew and in a little more than a hundred years, its population numbered fifty thousand people.

Norwegians have changed little with the passing of the years. In the year 1940, when Hitler's armies overran Norway, fearless young descendants of these very Vikings slipped away in small sailing ships which they skilfully navigated across the North Sea to Britain. Their bravery and their desire to be free were as great as those of their ancestors.

ERIC THE RED

Eric the Red was a famous Norse chief who was forced to leave Norway because he had committed a murder. He fled to the settlement in Iceland but the Icelanders would have none of him and he was forced to sail westward to find a new home for himself. Thus he came to the bleak shores of a great new island covered with ice and snow. To it he gave the name Greenland, "for," said he, "men will be more easily persuaded to come here if I give it a fair name." In a few years he returned to Iceland, where he obtained twenty-five ships, recruited eight hundred men and women, and took aboard some cattle. Because of storms at sea and damage from icebergs only fourteen ships arrived safely. Norsemen, however, liked this new land and as the years went by the settlement on it flourished.

Bjarni

Bjarni was a hardy Norse seaman who had left the colony in Iceland and roamed the seas for months looking

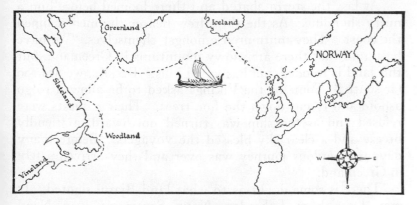

PATH OF THE VIKINGS

for plunder. As Yuletide drew near he thought of his home. He longed to sit beside his father's open hearth and talk over his adventures at sea. So the skilfully carved dragon's head on the prow of his long-ship was turned towards Iceland. The strong arms of his sailors tugged with a will on the oars. Days passed speedily. Each man thought of the fine young pig sizzling over the fire, of the sweet mead he would drink, and of the bright eyes of his loved ones whom he had not seen for many a day.

Disappointment awaited Bjarni, for, on reaching home, he received the news that his father, Herjulf, had migrated to the settlement of Eric the Red in Greenland. Careful sailing instructions were given to Bjarni and, undaunted, he set off for the land of snow-clad mountains.

Bad weather set in almost as soon as the ship took to sea. A drizzling rain, a leaden sky and a driving wind from the north, all helped to take him off his course. He was unable to get his bearings as he had not seen the sun, moon or stars for days and nights. The biting wind drove his ship on and on.

At last the storm abated and there loomed before him a misty shoreline. As the ship drew nearer the men scanned the coast. They murmured amongst themselves, "We have been told that there are snowy mountains in Greenland, but this land is wooded and has small hills. Besides, we are too far south." Some of the Vikings asked to be allowed to go ashore and to cut down the fine trees. Their requests were refused and as the ship was turned northward, a friendly breeze and a clear sky blessed the voyagers. Before many days the perilous journey was over and they arrived safely in Greenland.

There is some doubt as to what land Bjarni sighted. It may have been Labrador, Nova Scotia or even Newfoundland. This we do know, that Bjarni was the first European to see the eastern coast of North America.

Leif the Lucky

Thirteen years after Bjarni's return home, people had forgotten about his voyage. But one man remembered it. This was Leif, son of Eric the Red. Leif was a tall, strong, red-headed Viking, a born leader. He was determined to visit the land of which Bjarni had spoken. He bought Bjarni's ship and with a crew of thirty-five set out to sea.

In the ship were stored swords, axes, spears, shields and winged helmets, for who could tell what enemies might be encountered in these unknown lands?

For many a day Leif sailed on towards the south-west. He saw no land, only the surging waves beneath him and a friendly sky above. At last a long pencil line of coast was sighted. When Leif's men landed on this coast they found it was covered with flat grey stones. Fittingly, they named it Slateland. To-day we call it Labrador.

On again the long ship sailed till it came to a wooded shore. On landing, Leif and his men found tall trees, rich soil and fresh-water streams. Because wood is scarce in Iceland and Greenland, the Norsemen were happy to find these forests and to the land they gave the name Woodland. To-day it is called Newfoundland.

Setting sail again, after a few days, they reached a new and even more inviting shore. Here the rivers teemed with fine salmon. Tall trees towered up into the blue sky. Juicy purple grapes were found growing on vines in the woods. The Norsemen decided to rest here. Long low wooden houses were built. Thus the first white men to visit the shores of America spent the winter in the year 1000 A.D. To this land Leif gave the name Vineland.

What land was this? Leif reported that on the shortest day, the sun rose at seven-thirty and set at four-thirty. From this we can be fairly certain that it was somewhere in Eastern Canada or the North-eastern United States.

In the spring when Leif returned to Greenland everyone listened eagerly to the thrilling stories he had to tell. They agreed that a fitting name for him was Leif the Lucky. His brothers and a sister-in-law, the fair Gudrid, inspired by his tales, made several voyages to Vineland. Norse settlements were started there. There remains to this day what is believed to be a genuine record of these people. In the State of Massachusetts, U.S.A., there is a great stone on which is carved in the Runic symbols of the Norsemen these words, "Thorfinn (Leif's brother) with one hundred fifty-one Norsemen took possession of this land."

For some years the settlement flourished. After a time the natives became so unfriendly to the newcomers that many returned to their homeland. When the Black Death swept Europe in 1348, it took many lives in Greenland, and those left had little desire to travel to Vineland. The colony in North America dwindled and finally disappeared. Not until 1492 did the next Europeans sail to this new land. But the Norsemen must be regarded as the earliest discoverers of America.

TEST

Choose the correct word or words from the brackets in the following sentences:

1. Norsemen have (fair, dark) hair and (brown, blue) eyes.
2. The Norsemen loved (sailing, farming).
3. Norse ships were (long and low, high and broad).
4. A Viking ship had (one, three) sail (s).
5. Eric the Red started a Norse colony in (Iceland, Greenland).
6. The first Norseman to see the shores of America was (Bjarni, Leif the Lucky).
7. The land on which Leif first landed was (Woodland, Slateland).
8. Vikings found not only juicy grapes in Vineland but also (trees, gold).
9. In (1000 A.D., 1492 A.D.) Leif the Lucky spent the winter in America.
10. In the following years (no, many) Norsemen sailed to Vineland.

THINGS TO DO

1. Make a sketch of a Viking chieftain's helmet.
2. In plasticine make a model of a Viking ship showing oars, shields, sail.
3. On a map of Europe and North America mark out the route taken by Leif the Lucky on his famous voyage.
4. Imagine yourself a Viking chieftain who voyaged with Leif the Lucky and tell of some of the strange things you saw in Vineland.

BOOKS TO READ

FOR THE TEACHER

A History of Geographical Discovery and Exploration, J. N. Baker. *George G. Harrap & Co. Ltd.*

FOR THE PUPIL

The Book of Discovery, T. C. Bridges. *George G. Harrap & Co. Ltd.*

A Book of Seamen, F. H. Doughty. *Jonathan Cape Ltd.*

The Boy Through the Ages, D. M. Stuart. *George G. Harrap & Co. Ltd.*

Boy's Book of Exploration, J. Harris Gable. *E. P. Dutton & Co.*

By Star and Compass, W. S. Wallace. *Oxford University Press.*

Canada's Story, H. E. Marshall. *T. C. & E. C. Jack Ltd.*

Children of Odin, Padraic Colum. *Macmillan & Co.*

The Heroes of Asgard, A. & E. Keary. *Macmillan & Co.*

Stories of Exploration & Discovery, Arthur Archer. *Cambridge University Press.*

Tales from the Eddas, E. M. Wilmot-Buxton. *George G. Harrap & Co. Ltd.*

They Went Exploring, Arensa Sondergaard. *Harper & Bros.*

COLUMBUS

A little more than a hundred and fifty years after Marco Polo, from a prison cell in Genoa, wrote the story of his journeys, there lived in that same city a young, blue-eyed, red-haired boy named Christopher Columbus. Whenever a ship came into the harbour of Genoa from far-off lands, Columbus was to be seen standing on the dock watching the weather-beaten sailors unloading their cargoes. The lad was the son of a poor weaver. His father planned to make the boy follow the weaving trade, but young Columbus longed to be a sailor and to journey to the lands he had heard of from these seamen. When he grew a little older, he left his home and the weaving trade, and sailed off to sea.

One voyage Columbus made was to West Africa, another to England and a third to the foggy isle of Iceland where he heard sailors talk of a country far away across the western sea. These tales stirred his imagination and he planned to visit this land some day. When he returned to Portugal, where his brother Bartholomew lived, he told him all that he had heard. The two brothers studied many maps and a daring plan began to form in Christopher Columbus' mind. He believed that the earth was round like a ball and he felt certain that if he sailed westward across the Sea of Darkness, that he would come in a few weeks to land. What this land might be he did not know. Perhaps it would be Japan, Cathay or even India.

When Columbus tried to interest people in these ideas, however, they laughed and called him a dreamer. In those times, most men thought that if ships were to venture far from the coast into the unknown sea, great sea-monsters would swallow them together with their crew. Many men also claimed that the earth was flat and that ships reaching the end of the sea would fall over the edge of the world into space. The King of Portugal scoffed at Columbus and his plan, for Portugal at this time was more interested in finding a sea-route around Africa to India than in this westward route. Bartholomew Columbus journeyed to England to lay the plans before the ruler there but on the way his ship was attacked by pirates and he was delayed. For seven years, Christopher Columbus waited for some ruler to become interested and help him. During these weary years, his red hair turned white, his tall figure grew bent but he never lost faith in himself.

At last, although Ferdinand, the King of Spain, had refused to assist Columbus, his wife Queen Isabella became enthusiastic about his plans. She decided to pay for the ships and supplies herself. It is reported that she even sold her jewels in order to raise the needed money. Then King Ferdinand half-heartedly gave his consent and helped Columbus to get three ships, the *Santa Maria,* the *Nina* and the *Pinta.* These vessels were known as caravels. The *Santa Maria,* the largest of the three, was decked throughout but the other two had decks only at each end and were little more than open boats.

At that time men were afraid to sail out into the unknown sea and Columbus, though he promised rich rewards, had great difficulty in getting crews to man his ships. At last one hundred and twenty poorly-trained men were bribed to go on board. It is believed that many of these miserable fellows had been in jail and were promised their freedom if they would sail on this dangerous venture.

On a misty summer morning in August, 1492, the three ships with banners flying and drums beating sailed from Palos, Spain. The king promised that, if the voyage was successful, Columbus would be made an admiral, receive a pension for life, and be given a share of the riches **he** brought back. He was to take possession of the **islands or** lands that he might discover in the name of the King of Spain, and of these he was to be governor.

The great sails spread out and carried the ships, in six days, to the Canary Islands. There, fresh water, wood and meat were taken aboard and repairs were made to the rudder of the *Pinta*. Setting their course to the westward, they

FIRST VOYAGE OF COLUMBUS TO THE NEW WORLD

sailed out over the sparkling blue waves into the unknown. Days and weeks passed by and the sailors began to grow worried, for their supply of food was running low. Each day was taking them further away from home. When Columbus only laughed at their fears, they began to talk of taking control of the ships and turning them back to their homeland. One day they fancied they saw land to the westward; it was only a cloud on the horizon. As day after day passed with no sight of land, the crews complained more and more and Columbus, fearing open mutiny, was forced to put in chains anyone who disobeyed his orders. "Would your people in Spain not laugh at you if you returned without discovering new lands?" he asked. Even so the men grew more afraid and they talked of throwing Columbus into the sea.

One autumn morning, a sailor spied a carved piece of wood in the water. That afternoon, another sailor fished up a branch of a tree from the sea. These welcome discoveries raised the hopes of the men, for now they felt that land was near. Columbus promised a fine suit of velvet and a rich reward of money to the first man who should see

THEY APPROACHED A BEAUTIFUL GREEN ISLAND

land. Next day a bunch of red berries and a strange land plant were seen in the ocean. These were all good omens, and were brought proudly to Columbus. As darkness came on, few sailors felt like sleeping. Most of them stood on the decks peering out into the night for some sign of land. About two o'clock in the morning a light glimmered far to the west, as if a lighted torch was being carried by some one on shore. The hours till morning seemed long in passing. At dawn, a seaman on the *Pinta* joyfully signalled that he saw some low, sandy hills.

That very day, October twelfth, they approached a beautiful green island on which they saw people running about among the palm trees. The boats were quickly lowered. Wearing a splendid green velvet cloak and holding the flag of Spain aloft, Columbus stepped on shore after a voyage of thirty-five days. He firmly believed that this island was off the coast of Asia and that he had spanned the western ocean and found a new route to the rich lands of the East. A hymn of thanksgiving was sung by the men and all of them threw themselves on their knees and praised God for His goodness to them. Columbus took possession of the land in the name of the monarch, and to it he gave the name San Salvador; (to-day it is known as Watling Island). The crew crowded around their leader and begged forgiveness for their lack of faith in him and their bad behaviour on the voyage.

The brown-skinned natives on the island were shy at first, but, when they found the strangers peaceful, they came out from hiding places and thronged around the Spaniards gazing in wonder at their light skins, their dark beards and splendid clothes. Because Columbus believed he had reached islands off the coast of India, he gave the name Indians to these copper-coloured people and that name is still given to the natives of the Americas. Red caps, bells, glass beads and jugs were given to the Indians to win their friendship and in return the white men were given spices, parrots, darts, cotton thread and pieces of gold.

Finding no cities on this island, only green forests and yellow huts, Columbus sailed on in search of the land of India. When he put ashore at a place called *Cuba* by the natives, Columbus thought this was surely the land belonging to Kubla Khan's descendants. Again he was mistaken. He tells us that in Cuba, men went about with fire-brands in their mouths, made from rolling certain leaves into sticks, lighting them and smoking them. This was tobacco. Columbus little knew that men in the New World would grow richer by raising tobacco than by mining gold.

On the island of Haiti the Spaniards heard of gold mines to the west and plans were made to journey there. However Columbus was forced to change his plans. The *Santa Maria* ran ashore on a sandbank, turned over on her side and was wrecked. Food and clothing were saved and heaped on the beach, timber from the ship was used to build a fortress. Pinzon on the *Pinta*, a few weeks before, had gone off, hoping to be the first to come to the land of gold. Columbus had only one ship left. He was forced to make plans to return to Spain. There was not room for all the men on the little *Nina*, so thirty-eight sailors were left in the fortress. Then the ship set sail for Spain taking on board six Indians, spices, cotton, brightly-coloured parrots and enough gold to interest the King of Spain.

Just as the *Nina* set out, Pinzon returned with his ship. He had found no gold. He was quickly forgiven by Columbus and the two ships sped on their way back to Spain. All went well for a few days when a fierce storm and heavy seas parted the ships. Wave after wave broke over the tiny *Nina* and the crew gave themselves up for lost. Thinking the end was near, Columbus wrote the story of his voyage on a piece of parchment, put it into a water-tight cask and tossed it overboard, hoping that it would finally reach the shores of Europe and that men there would know of the success of his journey. All of the crew hoped that, by some miracle, God would spare their lives. At last the waves grew calm; not far away lay the Azore Islands. Here the ships were repaired, supplies of food were put on board and the dangers of the journey were nearly over as the ships made their way back home.

Seven months after setting out Columbus returned to Spain. Excited crowds rushed down to the harbour to welcome back the brave men who had crossed the fierce Atlantic Ocean. A great procession was held in the capital city of Seville. Thousands thronged the streets to view with wonder the six Indians in their native costumes, the birds with their bright plumage and the great admiral mounted on a snow-white horse. When the parade was over, Columbus was ushered into the throne room in the king's palace. He bowed humbly before Ferdinand and Isabella but the delighted monarch took him by the hand and led him to a special seat of honour between their thrones. There Columbus told the story of his journey. Ferdinand felt sure that Columbus had reached islands off the east coast of the continent of Asia.

In six months Columbus set off again for the west on his second voyage. This time money poured in, and hundreds of men clamoured to be allowed to accompany him. Fifteen hundred sailors, soldiers, farmers and missionaries were chosen to journey on the seventeen fine caravels. On this voyage a more southerly route was taken and the ships in due time arrived at a little island which the Spaniards named Dominica. Here the natives treated the white men to a luscious fruit, the juicy pineapple. Columbus and his men were the first Europeans to taste this fruit. One day in a native village Columbus discovered that the natives had other less tempting food; human arms and legs were being roasted over a fire and he realized that these fine-looking Carib Indians were cannibals.

The fortress Columbus had left behind on the island of Haiti was a mass of ruins when he returned to it and the thirty-eight Spaniards were dead. Later he learned that they had treated the Indians in a shocking manner and had been killed by them. Another good harbour was chosen and near it the town of Isabella was founded.

Sailing in search of gold and the passage to India, Columbus discovered the lovely island of Jamaica. When he became ill with fever he returned to Haiti to recover. The settlers were dissatisfied with their new land and grew quarrelsome. Many had come here believing that they could grow rich overnight without doing a great amount of work. When things did not turn out as they had expected they blamed their leader, Columbus. Sick as he was, Columbus dealt with the troublemakers firmly and as a result he made many enemies.

When Columbus returned to Spain no great welcome awaited him, for news of unrest and trouble had already reached Spain and people were disappointed when he returned with yams, cotton and Indian corn instead of piles of gold.

King Ferdinand and Queen Isabella however still had faith in Columbus and sent him out on his third voyage with six ships. This time he was advised to take a more southerly course. Trinidad was the name given to the first island that Columbus sighted. Oysters abounded in the waters around the island and parrots as large as hens were seen amongst the groves of graceful towering palm trees. Nearby a great current of fresh water from a mighty river poured into the sea and nearly sank the Spanish ships. This current was from the Orinoco, the second largest river in South America. Without knowing it, Columbus had reached the coast-line of South America, a great new continent.

Sailing on to Haiti, Columbus again found trouble and treachery at work. Jealous Spaniards seized Columbus, put him in chains and placed him on board a ship bound for Spain. On his return, Queen Isabella broke into tears when she heard how cruelly the snowy-haired explorer had been treated. She ordered his pardon and release.

In 1502, Columbus although tired and aged set out on

his fourth and most disastrous voyage. Reaching the coast of Central America, he sailed along the shore as far as Panama, still searching for the Spice Islands and India. From the first bad luck followed Columbus. The ships became leaky, the crews proved troublesome and Columbus fell ill. He was forced to return home where he found that his good friend, Queen Isabella, was dead. Nobody seemed to care about this penniless, bent old man. "After twenty years of toil and peril," he says in his diary, "I do not own even a roof in Spain." His home was a bare, cheerless attic. There, a short time after his return, he grew very ill and died, without knowing that his voyage had added two great new continents to the map of the world.

The great new world which Columbus discovered does not even bear his name. It was named for an explorer, Amerigo Vespucci, who sailed to the new land five years after Columbus made his famous voyage in 1492.

TEST

Choose the word or words that will make the statement correct.

1. Columbus thought that the world was
   —flat
   —round.
2. He planned to reach India by sailing
   —south
   —west.
3. The ruler who gave him help was
   —Queen Isabella
   —Queen Elizabeth.
4. Columbus' first voyage across the Atlantic took
   —five weeks
   —one week.

5. On this voyage Columbus had
   —six ships or caravels
   —three ships or caravels.
6. The first island which Columbus reached was
   —San Salvador
   —Jamaica.
7. When Columbus returned to Spain he brought back
   —cottons and parrots
   —rubies and diamonds.
8. On a later voyage Columbus discovered
   —Philippine Islands
   —Trinidad.

THINGS TO DO TOGETHER

1. Plan a class play with three characters, Columbus, King Ferdinand and Queen Isabella. Columbus is trying to prove to King Ferdinand that the earth is round.
2. Make a list of five things which Columbus brought back from the West Indies. Make a list of five things which he would have brought back with him if he had reached the East.
3. In plasticine, model a scene showing Columbus' three caravels at sea. Use blue plasticine for the water, brown plasticine for the ships, wooden sticks for the masts and white paper for the sails.

THINGS TO DO SEPARATELY

1. Make a booklet on "Let's Visit the West Indies". Show some of the interesting things you would see there, for example, palm trees, bananas, cotton, sponges, beaches. Tell what the people of the West Indies do to earn a living.
2. Often there are hurricanes in the West Indies. What harm do hurricanes do?

BALBOA

Columbus had hoped that his voyage would lead him to
the rich lands of Cathay and India. Instead, he had discovered the West Indies. Many Spaniards followed him to
sail up and down the coast of America searching for a passage to India. They had no idea of what lay beyond the
shores of the great new continent of America.

In a Spanish settlement on the island of Haiti, one of
the islands in the West Indies, there lived a bold, adventurous man, Balboa by name. Balboa was in debt to many
people and according to Spanish law in Haiti, he must
remain on the island till his debts were paid. Balboa wished
to escape and seek his fortune elsewhere.

One morning, seeing a ship loading supplies in the harbour, he thought of a clever plan of escape. The sailors
were carrying bread casks on board ship and into one of
these Balboa crept and hid. In a few hours the ship sailed
from the harbour and the shores of Haiti were left far
behind. For some days, the stowaway remained hidden in
the cask.

Stiff and tired, he broke out from his hiding-place and
presented himself before the captain who was so angry with
Balboa that he threatened to leave the unlucky man on a
desert island. However, a storm arose and the ship was
wrecked on a rock. Balboa with many other survivors was
cast ashore on the coast of a part of the mainland that
Balboa knew well. He led the party to the mouth of a river
named by the native Indians, the Darien. Here the
Spaniards decided to stay, for the land was rich and there
was plenty of fresh water. Needing provisions, the Spaniards fell fiercely on a nearby Indian village and stole from
it supplies of food, bales of cotton and a great quantity of
gold. Because Balboa was a good leader and a brave
fighter he became the first governor of the colony. Soon he

and his men began trading in gold with the Indians. He did not then know that this tiny colony stood on the narrow neck of land, the isthmus of Panama, which joins North and South America.

The Spaniards were greedy for gold. From the Indians they learned of a great kingdom which lay across the mountains and beyond the seas, where kings ate and drank from golden dishes. One of the chiefs declared that the journey to this land would take the Spaniards only a few days and that he would guide them across the mountains to the sea and to the land a few days journey down the coast.

Balboa and two hundred Spaniards set out. Only a few miles could be covered each day, for the journey led through deep swamps and steaming tropical jungles. Murderous Indians lay hidden in the branches of the trees and showered down poisonous arrows on those who were not on the alert. Many of the Spaniards became exhausted and fell down by the wayside, others grew ill with fever. The Spaniards were so eager to get the treasures that lay ahead that they left their sick comrades behind to die.

After many days of journeying, the party reached low hills and mountains. The tired men struggled up the mountain-side. Near the top, Balboa bade his men stop while he went on alone. From the bare peak, he gazed down on the blue surface of a vast ocean, its waves sparkling in the bright sunlight. Calling to the others to join him, Balboa quickly fell to his knees and thanked God for helping him to discover this Great South Sea. The men set up a rough wooden cross in a pile of stones to mark the place from which they had first seen the great sea.

Balboa hurried down the tree-covered slope and across the sands and plunged knee-deep into its waters. With his sword in one hand and the Royal Standard of Spain in the other, he claimed the sea, its islands and all the land around it for Spain. Two canoes were hauled to the water's edge and the Spaniards pushed off the shore. They were the first white men to sail from America on this ocean. The Indians on the coast traded gold and pearls; in return the Spaniards gave them worthless trinkets and bells. When the Indians told the white men of a land to the south which was rich in gold, Balboa was sure that it must be the land of India.

Balboa returned overland to his settlement at Darien bringing with him news of the vast new ocean and the land of gold. He began to make plans to build ships to sail on the mighty sea and explore its waters. His plans however were never carried out. A jealous leader in the colony had Balboa brought to court and tried on a charge of treating the natives cruelly. Balboa was condemned and publicly executed.

WITH SWORD IN ONE HAND AND THE ROYAL STANDARD OF SPAIN IN THE OTHER

TEST

Tell which of the following statements are true and which are false.

1. After Balboa was shipwrecked he and the other survivors made their way to Darien on the Isthmus of Panama.
2. The natives at Darien told Balboa of a land of gold which lay across the mountains.
3. Balboa and two hundred Spaniards had to journey over a desert to reach this land.

4. On the way there, friendly natives gave them help and supplies of food.
5. When Balboa had journeyed over the mountains he reached a great body of water which he named the Great South Sea.
6. Balboa claimed this sea for Spain.
7. From the natives here he received quantities of pearls.
8. Balboa never reached the land of gold.

THINGS TO DO TOGETHER

1. Sketch a scene showing Balboa with his sword in one hand and the flag of Spain in the other hand, plunging into the waters of the Great South Sea and claiming them for his country.
2. Discuss the building of the Panama Canal.

THINGS TO DO SEPARATELY

1. Collect pictures of the Panama Canal.
2. Find out from what two diseases the white men who helped to build this canal suffered.
3. How was the spread of these two diseases prevented?

THE CABOTS

John Cabot was a merchant seaman living in Bristol in England who, like Columbus, had dreamed of finding a new sea-route to the East by travelling west over the Atlantic. Also, like Columbus he was an Italian by birth and during his childhood he too had lived in Genoa. He had sailed to the Holy Land where he had traded with caravan leaders and had seen the spices, perfumes, silks and precious stones from India and China. When he asked where the caravan drivers had obtained these priceless riches they replied, "We do not know, but caravans come to our homes from distant countries to the east of us with this merchandise and the merchants tell us that it is brought to them from places still

further east." Cabot determined that one day he would
find a new route to these distant lands. Like many men of
that time, he felt sure that the earth was round and that by
travelling west, he would eventually reach China, Japan
and India. He hoped that his route would be a shorter one

ICEBERGS CAUSED THE CREW MANY SLEEPLESS HOURS

and perhaps less costly than that taken over the deserts,
plains and mountains by the old caravan roads. Visions of
the great piles of riches that would one day be his helped
to inspire him and carry him through much discouragement.

When news came to England of Columbus' voyage to
the West Indies, merchants there were anxious to send an
English vessel to the west to open up a sea-route to India.
Cabot and his son Sebastian were chosen to command this
expedition. Help was willingly given Cabot; a ship, ropes,
sails and all the necessary supplies were soon ready for the
voyage. King Henry VII granted permission to Cabot "to
sail to all parts, countries and seas of the East, and of the
West and of the North," and to occupy all these lands for

England in the name of the king. One fifth of all the profits of the voyage were to be paid to the king. Early in May 1497, Cabot set sail with a crew of eighteen seamen on board the vessel *Matthew*.

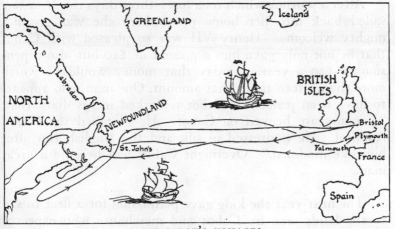

JOHN CABOT'S VOYAGES

As the little ship ploughed through the mighty waves, great schools of fish swarmed around her bows. At times, it was reported by the seamen, there were so many that they hindered the progress of the ship. Drifting icebergs and fog caused the crew to spend many sleepless hours on watch. In early June, the shores of a barren, lonely-looking country were sighted to which the Latin name *Prima Vista* was given. We now believe that the land sighted by Cabot was either Newfoundland or Cape Breton Island, but Cabot thought it was North-eastern Asia. Going ashore, the sailors saw no natives, but they did find snares to catch game and bone needles used in the making of nets. Cabot also saw trees bearing notches made by axes. White bears which ate fish, and partridges and eagles were also seen in great numbers, as Cabot travelled north in his ship along a

bleak and desolate shore, probably Labrador. Supplies were
running low, and as autumn was approaching, Cabot wisely
decided to return home before the cold weather and wintry
winds came.

After a journey which took forty-three days the *Matthew*
sailed back into her home port where she was given a
mighty welcome. Henry VII was so pleased with Cabot
that he not only gave him a present of £10 but also a pension of £20 a year. To-day that money would be worth
more than fifteen times that amount. One man who appears
to have been jealous of Cabot remarked in his diary that,
"Honours are heaped on Cabot. He is called the Grand
Admiral. He is dressed in silk and the English run after
him like madmen." Overnight Cabot had become a great
man.

The next year the king gave permission for a fleet to sail
to the lands seen by Cabot and merchants who expected
great wealth from trade with Cathay helped to outfit
several ships. Little is certain about this second voyage, for
Cabot did not keep a log-book telling of the daily happen-
ings on board ship, but some old and fairly trustworthy
records tell that about three hundred men sailed with Cabot
on his six ships. When Newfoundland was reached Cabot
made friends with the natives who offered him rich furs in
exchange for such trifles as bells and caps. Cabot returned
to Britain with the holds of his ships well filled with fish
and furs. He, however, received a luke-warm welcome for
the merchants expected rich spices, silks and jewels. John
Cabot made no more voyages and he died in 1499, a broken-
hearted and ruined man.

His son, Sebastian, continued to try and find a passage
to the East. Accounts of his voyages must be taken with a
grain of salt for he was a conceited man and some of his

statements were found to be exaggerated. We can be fairly sure however, that he made another voyage to Labrador and might even have entered Hudson Strait and Hudson Bay. In later years when he was older, he became an advisor to other explorers. He knew the waters of the North Atlantic very well. The King of England made him Grand Pilot at a salary of £166, 13s, 6d a year. It was Sebastian Cabot who suggested that every ship should keep a log or daily account of her course and a record of the new lands visited.

Although the Cabots did not find a route to the East, they did discover a source of great wealth for England. Cod-fishing off the Grand Banks of Newfoundland provided English fishermen with a livelihood for hundreds of years. Valuable furs, mink, beaver and fox from Eastern Canada were shipped each year to England and they too were a great source of wealth. In time the fish and furs were far more important than the spices that Cabot had so greatly desired to bring back. The great island of Newfoundland, which Cabot found, was the first of Britain's colonies overseas and gave her a claim to land in the New World.

TEST

Complete each sentence begun in the left-hand column by choosing its proper ending from the right-hand column.

1. Cabot set sail from   (*a*) eighteen sailors
2. His plan was to find   (*b*) Newfoundland or Cape Breton Island.
3. He had a crew of   (*c*) fish and furs
4. While he was at sea, Cabot saw   (*d*) log-books
5. The land Cabot reached was probably (*e*) Sebastian
6. Cabot's son who also made several voyages was called   (*f*) Bristol, England

7. The Cabots brought back quantities (*g*) a shorter route to
   of   the East
8. After the journeys of the Cabots, (*h*) icebergs
   all British sailing ships were re-
   quired to keep

THINGS TO DO TOGETHER

1. On a map showing Europe, the Atlantic Ocean and North
   America, mark the route which John Cabot took on his first
   voyage. Locate the following places on your map: Bristol,
   England, Atlantic Ocean, Newfoundland, Cape Breton Island
   and Labrador.
2. Write a paragraph of about seven or eight sentences, telling
   of John Cabot's first journey. Try to use these words in your
   account: Bristol, *Matthew*, icebergs, schools of fish, Newfoundland, Grand Admiral of the Fleet.

THINGS TO DO SEPARATELY

1. Find out how much of an iceberg shows above the surface of
   the water and how much is hidden from view.
2. What is the work of the Iceberg Patrol along the coasts of
   Nova Scotia, Newfoundland and Labrador?
3. Make a list of at least five kinds of fur which Canadian furriers
   send to other countries.

BOOKS TO READ

For the Teacher

    Great Navigators and Discoverers, J. A. Brandon. *George G.
Harrap & Co. Ltd.*

    A History of Geographical Discovery and Exploration, J. N.
Baker. *George G. Harrap & Co. Ltd.*

For the Pupil

    America Then and Now, Edna McGuire. *Macmillan & Co.*

    The Book of Discovery, T. C. Bridges. *George G. Harrap &
Co. Ltd.*

A Book of Seamen, F. A. Doughty. *Jonathan Cape Limited*.
Boy's Book of Exploration, J. Harris Gable. *E. P. Dutton & Co*.

By Star and Compass, W. S. Wallace. *Oxford University Press*.
Heroes of Discovery, R. J. Finch. *University of London Press*.
Map Makers, J. Cottler and H. Jaffe. *George G. Harrap & Co. Ltd*.

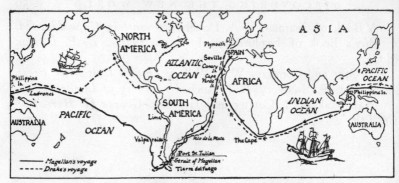

ROUTES OF MAGELLAN AND DRAKE

III. CIRCUMNAVIGATING THE GLOBE

MAGELLAN

ON a hot August morning in the year 1519, five ships set
sail from a seaport in Spain. They were manned by a
crew of two hundred and thirty-seven sailors and were
commanded by a Portuguese captain, Ferdinand Magellan.
The purpose of the voyage was to reach the great new ocean
which Balboa had sighted, to cross it and to reach India and
the Spice Islands. The King of Spain had provided the
ships, the crew, and supplies for two years, and had
promised Magellan one-twentieth of all the profits from the
voyage. In the holds of the ships were great quantities of
bells, mirrors, knives, scarlet cloth and combs to help the
Spaniards make friends with the new peoples that they met
on the way.

Magellan steered his course south-west across the Atlantic Ocean. He planned to sail along the coast of South
America till he found a channel through to the Great South
Sea. The flagship, *Trinidad,* carried a torch on her high
stern to enable the other ships, following behind to see her
in the darkness. Magellan's words to the other captains
were, "Follow the flagship and question not."

60

At first the sea was calm and the sun, blazing down on the decks of the ships, was so hot that it caused the tar to bubble between the seams of wood. This was followed by two months of fierce storms and gales which tore away the sails and tossed the ships wildly about on the waves. The sailors began to grow fearful and many wished to turn back. Two of the captains planned to get rid of Magellan and take over command of the fleet. They said of Magellan, "This limping Portuguese foreigner is leading us to our deaths."

At last the palm-fringed shore of Brazil was reached. Magellan sailed south along the coast searching for an opening which would lead into the new ocean. Past bays and river mouths the fleet sailed. From time to time parties of sailors were sent ashore to bring back supplies of meat, fruit and vegetables; other parties were sent out to explore the water openings along the coast. If the water in these inlets was fresh the seamen knew that the opening was a river and not the channel for which they were searching. The sailors traded with the natives; for a knife they received five chickens, for a comb fresh fish for ten men and for a red cap a basket of fresh fruit.

When they had travelled far to the south the weather became bitterly cold. Magellan decided to rest in a quiet bay during the winter months. To this harbour he gave the name Port St. Julian. Here trouble began to brew. The discontented sailors wanted to go back to Spain. When Magellan refused, plans were made to kill him but he, hearing of the plot, quickly arrested the leaders. "Put the mutinous dogs in irons and see that you guard them well," he commanded. Two of the rebels were executed, two others were left on a lonely bleak shore to die. By this quick action, Magellan showed the others that he was capable, strong and ruthless and no more mutinies broke out.

So far no natives had been sighted in this region. One day towards the end of the winter a great savage-looking giant dressed in skins and carrying a great bow and a quiver of long arrows came running along the shore. The giant pointed to the sky for he thought that these white men were gods who had come down to earth from heaven. One of the sailors, an Italian, who kept a diary tells us that this native was so tall "we reached only to his waist." Later other natives came along the shore. Some went out to the Spanish ships. A writer described one of the giants in these words: "His face was large and painted red all over, while about his eyes he was painted yellow; and he had two hearts painted on the middle of his cheeks. His scanty hair was painted white. He was dressed in the skins of animals skilfully sewn together." When one native saw himself in a mirror for the first time, he was so surprised that he jumped backwards, knocking down four Spaniards who were standing near. The feet of these natives were so big that the sailors called them Patagonians which in Spanish means "big feet" and their country to this day is called *Patagonia*. Their appetites were very large. At one meal a giant ate several live rats, skins, tails and all, a basketful of sea-biscuits, and washed it all down with a bucket of water.

When the winter was over the ships, now only four in number, for one had been wrecked, set out again. At last they came to a narrow channel of salt water into which they sailed. Carefully they made their way through the curving, twisting strait. Black sullen hills lay on either side. The sun rarely shone. High snow-capped mountains lay on their right and great glaciers of snow flowed down between the mountains into the dark waters of the channel. On the hill-tops of the land to the south, fires burned all night long, but no natives were seen. The fires were kept burning all the time because the natives did not know how to light the fires should they ever go out. To this land the Spaniards gave the name *Tierra del Fuego* meaning The Land of Fire.

ON EITHER SIDE LAY BLACK SULLEN HILLS

For over a month Magellan sailed through these dangerous waters. Many of the sailors begged Magellan to turn back but he was firm and determined to go on. He said, "If we have to eat the leather on the ship's yards yet we will go on." When a great calm ocean came into view, the sailors breathed sighs of relief and some wept for joy. They had found the Great South Sea which Balboa had discovered and which they believed led to the Spice Islands and India. This passage which leads from the Atlantic Ocean to the Pacific was named the Strait of Magellan.

As the days passed the sea continued so calm and quiet that it was decided to call it the Pacific which means "peaceful". Only three ships now remained. While passing through the Strait of Magellan, the commander of one ship had grown fearful and returned home to Spain. Weeks and months passed. More hardships lay in store for the sailors. Supplies of food and water ran low. Much of the food that remained turned bad and the water supply was tainted. The crew ate biscuits turned to dust and filled with worms. Leather from the masts was soaked for four days to soften it up and then made into a stew. Even the rats which were thin and bony were eaten by the starving men. On this diet the men grew weak from hunger and disease. Some of the crew died of starvation, many more suffered from scurvy. Two or three islands were sighted but there was no living thing on them, no food, no water, only rocks. All this time the sun shone brightly and the sea remained quiet.

One morning land was sighted. Brown-skinned natives came aboard bringing sweet potatoes, bananas, flying fish and pork to the starving men. With a change in diet the crew soon recovered. Meanwhile the natives swarmed over the ship and stole all the small things they could take, nails, knives, mirrors and forks, and as they had no pockets, they hid their loot in their fuzzy black hair. They were such thieves that Magellan named their islands *Ladrones* or Robbers' Isles. Guam is the largest of the Ladrones.

Leaving the Ladrones, the ships sailed on till they came to a group of islands which were later named the Philippines. Magellan claimed them for the King of Spain. Here many of the natives were converted to Christianity. Magellan made friends with a ruler of one of these isles, the King of Zebu. This brown-skinned monarch had thick black hair and wore big gold ear-rings and a golden dagger in his silk embroidered loin cloth. Magellan gave him a fine yellow Turkish robe and a red cap. The king invited Magellan to his palace which was a thatched barn built on posts with a bamboo ladder for a stairway. The two men sat cross-legged on straw mats and ate roasted fish, ginger, rice and pork.

From the King of Zebu, Magellan learned of another ruler, hostile to the king. With a party of three boatloads of Spaniards and a thousand natives in large war canoes, Magellan set out to bring this king to terms. In the battle that followed, the Spaniards fought bravely, but they were hopelessly outnumbered. In the midst of the fight, Magellan was wounded in the leg by a bamboo spear and he fell into the water where he was savagely attacked and stabbed to death. His men fled in panic back to their boats. They were now without a leader. Later one of his followers wrote of him: "Thus perished Magellan, our guide, our light, and our support."

Leaderless now, the expedition set out for the Spice Islands. Of the three remaining ships, one was so unseaworthy she had to be burned, the timbers of the second one were so rotten that it did not dare attempt the long journey home and the only one that remained was the *Victoria*, the smallest of the fleet of five ships that had left Spain. A precious cargo of cloves, cinnamon and nutmeg was stored in her hold and she set out for Spain. Of the crew of two hundred and forty men only forty-seven remained. Not all of these were to return to Spain. Even though the ship had taken on food for six months, much of it went bad. Leaks appeared in the timbers of the *Victoria* and day after day was spent in pumping out the water from her holds. When the tiny ship reached Spain only eighteen gaunt starving survivors remained.

The voyage had taken three years. It had cost the lives of Magellan and over two hundred men, but the survivors had sailed around the globe and so had proved that the earth was not flat. Map-makers revised their maps and added to them the Strait of Magellan, the vast Pacific Ocean, and the Philippine Islands.

TEST

From the brackets choose the correct word or group of words to complete each sentence.

1. Magellan was sent out on a voyage of exploration by the King of (Spain, Portugal).
2. Magellan's task was to search for a water passage from the (Atlantic to the Pacific Ocean, Atlantic to the Indian Ocean).
3. *Tierra del Fuego* means (Land of Ice, Land of Fire).
4. Magellan named the great new ocean into which he sailed the Pacific because it was so (peaceful, stormy).
5. During the voyage across the Pacific Ocean, Magellan's men suffered from (frost-bite, hunger).
6. Magellan was killed soon after the expedition reached (Philippine Islands, India).
7. The only ship which returned to its home port after the voyage around the world was the (*Trinidad, Victoria*).
8. This ship brought back a cargo of (spices, gold).

THINGS TO DO TOGETHER

1. On a long sheet of brown wrapping paper show scenes from the story. Use charcoal and coloured chalk. Here are some suggestions:
   (1) The Patagonian peering into the mirror which Magellan gave to him.
   (2) Magellan's ships sailing through the dangerous waters of the Strait of Magellan.
   (3) The natives of the Philippine Islands attacking Magellan.
2. Imagine that several of you are sailors from the only vessel that returned home after the long voyage. You are being questioned by the king. Tell him why many of your fellow crew members did not return home with you.

THINGS TO DO SEPARATELY

1. Collect pictures of tropical fruits. Label them and display them on your bulletin board.
2. Collect pictures of the Philippine Islands. Paste them in your Social Studies Scrap Book.

DRAKE

From slave-trader and roving pirate to Admiral of the Fleet in the navy of Good Queen Bess, that was the ascent in the ladder of success made by Francis Drake. He was the man who humbled Spain, then mistress of the seas. He was also the first Englishman to sail around the world.

Drake, son of a God-fearing minister, took to sea at an early age. He and John Hawkins engaged in selling negro slaves to the Spaniards in the West Indies. The negroes, whom Drake brought from West Africa, were sold to work on the sugar plantations. In exchange Drake received hides, ginger, sugar, pearls, gold and silver.

After a time Spain began to resent British seamen sailing in Spanish waters in the West Indies. On Drake's third slave-trading voyage, Hawkins' ships were damaged during a hurricane and were permitted to enter a Spanish harbour in Mexico for repairs. Although the Spaniards promised not to harm them, they broke their word and treacherously fired on the English ships. Three were lost; only the two smallest limped back home. When the battered ships returned, Drake vowed that he would avenge the wrong done to Hawkins and himself by the Spanish.

For the next few years, Drake scouted through the waters of the West Indies studying the routes of the great treasure-laden galleons travelling from the Spanish Main back home to Spain. He learned, too, the routes taken by ships bringing gold and silver from mines in Peru up the Pacific coast to Panama where the treasure was transferred from the ships to mule-trains which carried it overland to a port on the Atlantic side. Drake was looking for any way in which he might take his revenge upon the Spaniards. When he sailed along a new coast-line or up a channel the path he followed was charted in his mind forever.

After years of preparation, he at last put his plan into action. He made his headquarters at a little secret base near Panama which he named Port Pheasant. From here, he made daring attacks on Spanish galleons, on Spanish ports and on mule-trains carrying the treasure overland. On one of these attacks, Drake was thrilled to gaze on a sight that no Englishman up to that time had ever seen. From a tree-top in Panama, he saw the vast Pacific Ocean. He vowed to sail on it and while there to seize any Spanish treasure ships that he might find.

To fulfil this vow Drake sailed from Plymouth harbour on November 15, 1577, in the greatest secrecy, with a little fleet of five ships, the *Pelican, Elizabeth, Marigold, Swan* and *Christopher*. With him sailed two hundred of England's finest seamen.

At first things went against Drake. A storm broke out in the English Channel and the ships were forced to return to harbour for repairs. In a month's time they started out again. Sailing in a southerly direction through the Atlantic Ocean, they reached, on Christmas Day, the Cape Verde Islands off the west coast of Africa. The trip across the Atlantic was a long one. It took fifty-four days. By turns the seas were rough and then calm.

Drake and his officers lived in great splendour. Drake's cabin contained fine oak furniture. At meal times he and his officers were served from silver dishes and musicians played for them on their fiddles. Drake said that wherever he went, men should admire the polished manners and high standard of living of English gentlemen.

THE GOLDEN HIND

One fair day, the coast of Brazil was sighted. The long days at sea were forgotten and Drake was able to go ashore, for he was anxious to learn more about this land. Further down the coast he put in at the Rio de la Plata where food was obtained. The winter months of June, July and August were spent at St. Julian. Here Magellan had wintered on his historic trip and here, too, he had been forced to execute a mutinous officer. History repeated itself for Doughty, one of Drake's captains, and his closest friend, was found to be a spy in the pay of Spain. He had been plotting to bring the voyage to disaster. At first Drake would not believe the reports that the other officers gave him regarding this charming rogue, but when he was at last convinced of Doughty's guilt, he had the traitor executed.

After a stay of several months in St. Julian the fleet sailed south. There were now only three ships for two had begun to leak and had been abandoned. When the Strait of Magellan was reached, Drake was amazed at the many turnings and twistings of the waterway and he marvelled at the tall, snowy mountain-peaks on either side of the channel. It was difficult, he found, to drop anchor owing to the great depth of the water. As the three ships proceeded through the strait, a fierce storm arose and the little *Marigold* sank with all hands. Thinking that the other ships were lost, the commander of the *Elizabeth* turned back to the Atlantic and safely made his way to England. Drake's ship, however, rode out the storm unharmed. At this time the *Pelican's* name was changed to the *Golden Hind* in honour of Sir Christopher Hatton, a close friend of Francis Drake, who had given money to build the ship and whose crest was a golden hind.

Drake, at last, reached the Pacific Ocean on which he had for so long wished to sail. Magellan had found the ocean a calm and peaceful one and had named it the Pacific. It proved far from peaceful for Drake and his men. Great storms arose, waves swept across the decks and the crew feared that the end was near for them. For nearly two months, the storm raged and lashed at the sails and rigging. Men could not tell day from night, so heavy and black were the clouds. The little *Golden Hind* was tossed about like a "ball in a racket". Blown far to the south, the ship was driven around Cape Horn at the southernmost tip of South America. Thus Drake made a very important discovery; he found that the land south of the Strait of Magellan was just a group of islands and was not attached to a great southern continent as had been thought up until this time. It was possible for a ship to sail from the Atlantic to the Pacific around Cape Horn instead of travelling through the dangerous straits. For the next fifty years, the British kept this discovery a closely-guarded secret.

When the weather cleared, the ship sailed north close to the western coast of America. One day the seamen spied an Indian in a canoe who told them that not far off was a great Spanish galleon laden with gold, emeralds and wine. It was the *Grand Captain of the South* and it lay in the harbour of Valparaiso. The Indian, who hated the Spaniards because of their cruelty to his countrymen, was glad to pilot the *Golden Hind* into the harbour. When Drake attacked, the Spaniards were completely taken by surprise. They had not dreamed of English ships appearing on the Pacific coast. With little difficulty, the treasure ship was captured and her precious cargo was put into the hold of the *Golden Hind*. Further up the coast an amusing incident happened. A Spaniard lay asleep on a hillside and beside him were lying thirteen bars of silver. Drake's men put to shore in a small boat, took the silver and left the Spaniard sleeping peacefully. On another occasion a landing party met a Spaniard and an Indian driving eight Peruvian sheep, each bearing two leathern bags of silver. These sheep were the llamas of Peru. From this caravan eight hundred pounds of silver were taken.

When Drake arrived at Lima, he learned that the *Cacafuego, The Glory of the South Sea,* one of the richest Spanish vessels had sailed from port fourteen days before and was headed for Panama. Drake offered a gold chain to the man who should first sight her. When the great ship hove into view, guns and cutlasses were brought on deck and the men made ready for action. In no time the English sailors were rushing over the sides of the great prize. The battle was short for, again, the Spaniards were taken by surprise. The proud Spanish captain said he would lay down his sword to no one but the Dragon or *El Draco* as the enemy called Drake. It took two days to count the treasure which this galleon carried. Her hold contained thirteen chests full of money, eighty pounds weight of gold and twenty-six tons of silver. One sailor remarked that the ship should not have been called the *Cacafuego* (Spitfire) but the *Cacaplata* (Spit-silver).

The news of Drake's attacks had travelled to all the Spanish harbours on the Pacific coast. Everywhere now

Spaniards were lying in wait for him, hoping for a chance to strike back at the daring pirate. The *Golden Hind* sailed on up the coast but no more galleons were found. She carried in her hold greater treasures than had ever before fallen to an English ship. With such a cargo, Drake began to think of returning home but he dared not go back the way he had come. The voyage home had to be made over another route. He therefore sailed on up the coast past Mexico and the United States as far as the island we now call Vancouver Island. He was seeking a passage leading through America to the Atlantic Ocean which would provide a short route home to England. Each day, however, the coast-line turned west and still further west. Icy winds from the lofty snow-capped mountains blew down on the little vessel. At last with regret Drake was forced to turn south again and seek another route home.

Provisions were running short and the sailors needed a rest, so when the *Golden Hind* reached a "fair and good baye", where San Francisco stands to-day, Drake decided to spend several months there. The natives treated the white men as gods and their king insisted on resigning his kingdom to the Great White God. Before leaving, Drake nailed a plate of brass to a post on which were engraved words which stated that the land was taken by him in the name of Good Queen Bess. To this place, Drake gave the name New Albion. After the ship was cleaned, repaired and stocked up with supplies, it set out in a westerly direction across the Pacific.

They sailed without sight of land for sixty-eight days. Stolen Spanish charts made the sailing easier. Drake's fine leadership kept the crew in order and their spirits high. At the first group of islands sighted, unfriendly natives drove the *Golden Hind* away. In a few days, the ship reached the Philippine Islands where the crew enjoyed luscious tropical fruits, fish, fowl, sweet potatoes and fresh water. At the Spice Islands, Drake was met by their king, who paid honour to the Englishman and treated him royally. Disaster nearly overtook the ship, however, for it struck a reef off one of these islands and remained fast for eight terrible hours. All hands thought the ship would be a total wreck. Luckily the wind changed, the vessel slipped off the coral ledge and refloated without suffering very serious damage. The voyage across the Indian Ocean to the Cape of Good Hope was quiet and uneventful. Drake would not allow his men to land there for he wished to get his rich cargo home to England without delay.

QUEEN ELIZABETH THEN KNIGHTED DRAKE

A few months later, the *Golden Hind* glided into the harbour of Plymouth, two years, ten months and some odd days after she had set out. Drake who had set out into the west had returned in triumph from the east bearing with him a cargo of great wealth. He had kept his vow and had humbled the Spaniards in their possessions on the Pacific coast of South America. The bells pealed out and the news ran through the town that Drake had come home. The *Golden Hind* travelled on to Deptford near London. On April 5, 1581, Queen Elizabeth boarded the ship, dined and heard Drake's story. She then knighted him on the quarter-deck of his ship.

At the Queen's command, the ship was kept as a national treasure. To-day if you visit the Bodleian Library in Oxford, England, you will see a fine oak chair made from the timbers of this famous ship.

TEST

In a sentence write an answer to each of the following questions:

1. Who was Queen of England when Drake set out on his famous voyage?
2. To what part of the world did Drake sail in order to attack Spanish towns and ships?
3. After Drake sailed through the Strait of Magellan what did he rename his ship, the *Pelican*?
4. What riches did Drake seize from the great Spanish galleons the *Cacafuego* and the *Grand Captain of the South*?
5. By what route did Drake return to England? Why?
6. How long did the complete voyage take?
7. What great honour did Drake receive when he returned home?

THINGS TO DO TOGETHER

1. Study pictures of costumes at the time of Francis Drake. Make a sketch showing an English gentleman of that time.
2. On a map trace the route of Drake's journey around the world. Be sure to show where the following important places are located: St. Julian, Strait of Magellan, Peru, New Albion, East Indies, Cape of Good Hope, England.

THINGS TO DO SEPARATELY

1. Read the story of Drake and the Spanish Armada.
2. Look for a copy of the famous picture entitled, *The Armada is in Sight*, showing Drake awaiting the arrival of the Spanish Armada.

BOOKS TO READ

For the Teacher

Exploration and Discovery, Arthur Archer. *Cambridge University Press.*

Unrolling the Map, Leonard Outhwaite. *McClelland & Stewart Ltd.*

For the Pupil

The Book of Discovery, M. B. Synge. *Thos. Nelson & Sons Limited.*

A Book of Famous Pirates, A. M. Smyth. *Oxford University Press.*

Heroes of Discovery, R. J. Finch. *University of London Press.*

Map Makers, J. Cottler and H. Jaffe. *Ryerson Press.*

Pilgrims and Adventurers, Part II, Phyllis Wragge. (Foundations of History, Book D). *Thos. Nelson & Sons Limited.*

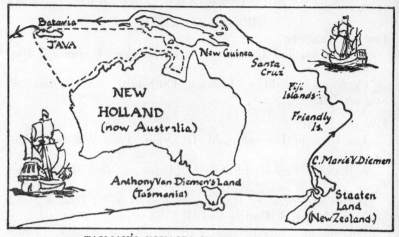

TASMAN'S VOYAGES IN THE SOUTH SEAS
1642 ——————— 1644 --------------

IV. DISCOVERIES IN THE SOUTH SEAS

ABEL TASMAN

FOR many years sailors in the South Seas had searched for a great continent which they believed existed far to the south of the East Indies. The Dutch, particularly, who had settled in Java were interested in this "Great South Land" as they called it, which, they thought, might be rich in gold and silver like the lands that the Spaniards had found in South America. The governor of the Dutch colonies in the East Indies, Anthony van Diemen, wished to find out if such a continent existed. He chose Abel Tasman, a Dutch sailor, to command an expedition of discovery.

In 1644, Tasman was given charge of two ships, the *Heemskerck* and the *Sea-hen*, and enough food to last for eighteen months. The vessels were carried first, by prevailing winds, in a south-westerly direction, towards Africa and then turned to the east. Great gales and rough rolling seas battered the ships about and did much damage, tearing the sails and breaking the rigging. The voyage was so long and terrible that Tasman offered a rich reward of money to the first sailor who should sight land of any kind. One morning, after three months at sea, one of the sailors

THE SHIP'S CARPENTER CLAIMED THE NEW LAND FOR HOLLAND

sighted a high rocky coast far off in the distance and some blue mountains rising out of the sea. As the ships approached the coast, the gales returned and, although several small boats tried to reach the shore, the heavy seas were too much for them and they were forced to return. The ship's carpenter volunteered to swim ashore and plant the flag of Holland on this new land. Fighting against the waves in a heavy sea, he reached the shore, hoisted the Dutch flag on a hill-top and took the new land in the name of the King of Holland. "As the land had not been known before to any European, we called it Van Diemen's Land," wrote Tasman in his log-book. To-day this land is known as

Tasmania in honour of its discoverer. Although Tasman did not know it, he had reached a large island, south-east of Australia. The man who had gone ashore saw no people, but he did see notches cut in the trunks of the trees, which must have been put there by human beings.

For nine days the ships continued in an easterly direction, until they sighted the tree-clad slopes of a fine new land. Natives in long, carved war-canoes came out, armed with sharp spears and clubs, and crowded around the Dutch ships. These strange men were of a colour between brown and yellow, their hair was long and thick and combed up into little knobs on the tops of their heads. Tasman was in great need of fresh water and food, but when he sent two row-boats, full of men, to shore to get supplies, these warlike natives, friendly at first, later attacked the sailors; three were killed and another was badly wounded.

The remaining sailors, badly frightened, returned to the ships without setting foot on these unfriendly shores. Because of the fierce attack on his men, Tasman named the inlet Murderer's Bay. The Dutch, for many years, called this new land Staaten Land and so it continued to be called until it was renamed New Zealand. Tasman sailed on northward, looking for a place to land, but the native Maoris proved to be so unfriendly that the Dutch did not dare to risk landing.

To the north of Staaten Land lay some beautiful tree-clad islands where tall, strong, black natives with mops of fuzzy hair gladly brought Tasman fish, fowl, fruits and fresh water as presents. These black men were so kind to the Dutch sailors that Tasman named their islands the Friendly Islands.

The *Heemskerck* and the *Sea-hen* coasted through more groups of islands till they reached the northern shores of a large island which is now New Guinea. The natives welcomed the Dutch and gave them thousands of coco-nuts as well as a hundred stalks of bananas. Journeying on to the west the two ships returned once more to the port on the island of Java from which they had sailed, after a journey of nine months.

TASMAN RECEIVED GIFTS OF COCO-NUTS AND BANANAS

Tasman unknown to himself had sailed around the continent of Australia, the Great South Land. The Governor, van Diemen, was greatly disappointed with Tasman because he had not explored these new lands thoroughly, and because he brought back no gold or silver, but Tasman explained that further exploration had been impossible because of the leaking condition of his ships, his lack of food and the war-like nature of the savages he had found in Staaten Land.

Two years later Tasman again set out to explore more of the Great South Land, to make maps of the capes, bays, inlets, rivers, reefs and sands that he passed, and also to trade with the natives. Little is known of this voyage, but it is known that he sailed along the north-western coast of what is to-day Australia; to it Tasman gave the name New Holland. Again he returned home without news of rich lands teeming with gold and silver and, as before, the Dutch Governor was keenly disappointed. Van Diemen lost interest in spending any more money on discovery, and the Dutch made no use whatever of the fine carefully-plotted maps that Tasman had made.

On the floor of the great Town Hall in the city of Amsterdam in Holland is to be seen to this day, inlaid in stone, "The complete map of the Southern Continent surveyed by Captain Abel Tasman". Although Tasman had sailed in the waters near Australia he never knew that Tasmania, New Zealand and New Guinea were islands. He believed that they were all part of one great southern continent.

TEST

Choose from the brackets the correct word or words to complete the following statements:

1. Tasman was born in (France, Holland, England).
2. The governor of Java sent Tasman on a voyage to try to find (a sea-route to Japan, the Great South Land, the South Pole).
3. When the ship's carpenter landed in Van Diemen's Land (Tasmania) he saw (many natives, few natives, no natives).
4. Tasman found out that the natives of Staaten Land (New Zealand) were (shy, friendly, fierce).
5. The natives of Staaten Land were (Bushmen, Negroes, Maoris).
6. The natives of New Guinea gave Tasman (coco-nuts and bananas, gold and silver, fish and furs).
7. Tasman returned to Java from his first voyage because (many of his men died of scurvy, his ships were in a leaky condition, he had a large cargo of gold).
8. On his second journey of discovery, Tasman explored the coast of (south-eastern New Holland, north-western New Holland, Staaten Land).

9. When Tasman returned from his second journey of discovery the governor of Java decided (to send Tasman on another journey, to take no further interest in the Great South Land, to make Tasman governor of the Great South Land).

10. To-day in Amsterdam, Holland there is a memorial in honour of Tasman. It is (a map inlaid in the floor of the Town Hall, a monument in the City Square).

THINGS TO DO TOGETHER

1. On a map of Australia and the neighbouring islands mark in the following:— Tasmania, New Zealand, Australia, Friendly Islands, New Guinea and Java. Mark in, using red crayon, Tasman's route on his first voyage and using blue crayon, Tasman's route on his second voyage.

2. Make an illustration showing the ship's carpenter swimming ashore to plant the flag of Holland on Van Diemen's Land.

THINGS TO DO SEPARATELY

1. Find out all that you can about the Maoris of New Zealand under the following headings (a) appearance (b) homes (c) boats (d) occupations.

2. Make a coloured picture of the flag of Holland.

3. What lands to-day belong to Holland (a) in South America (b) in Asia?

BOOKS TO READ

FOR THE TEACHER

Great Navigators and Discoverers, J. A. Brendon. *Geo. G. Harrap & Co. Ltd.*

Exploration and Discovery, Arthur Archer. *Cambridge University Press.*

A History of Geographical Discovery and Exploration, J. N. L. Baker. *Geo. G. Harrap & Co. Ltd.*

FOR THE PUPIL

A Book of Discovery, M. B. Synge. *Thos. Nelson & Sons.*

The Book of Discovery, T. C. Bridges. *Geo. G. Harrap & Co. Ltd.*

Captain James Cook

For over a hundred years after Tasman's voyages, no other explorer sailed to the waters around the Great Southern Continent. Little use, if any, was made of the fine maps and charts Tasman had made.

Over the seas in Britain, more than a hundred years after Tasman, lived a youth who was to carry on the work of exploration that Tasman had started. This English lad was James Cook. At the age of thirteen Cook left his job in a draper's shop and joined a coal ship. Life at sea in those days was hard and rough, but Cook loved ships. At the age of twenty-seven he joined the Royal Navy. In four years he rose steadily until he became captain of his ship. Then he spent some time surveying the River St. Lawrence. Here he proved himself to be one of the wisest captains of his day. Thus when the British government was searching for a suitable commander to take charge of an expedition to the South Pacific on an important mission, Captain James Cook was chosen as leader.

FIRST VOYAGE

This expedition was to Tahiti in the South Seas, there to observe a total eclipse of the sun. Cook was also given the important task of charting out any new lands or islands which he might visit. He was instructed to watch and care for the health of his sailors and, if possible, keep them fit and well. In those days, when ships went to sea on long voyages, sailors fell ill with a disease called scurvy. Very often three out of four sailors died from this terrible sickness. Cook believed scurvy was brought on by a lack of fresh fruits, vegetables and meats in the diet. He was determined to do all that he could to prevent this sickness among his men. Therefore he took large quantities of malt, mustard, vinegar, wheat, orange and lemon juice and dried fruit on board. Plans were made to stop wherever it was possible, to get extra supplies of fresh food.

From England his ship, the *Endeavour,* sailed south through the Atlantic Ocean and on to Tahiti. This was a beautiful palm-fringed island bathed in warm tropical sunshine. The natives of Tahiti were handsome, tall and strong,

COOK MADE FRIENDS WITH THE NATIVES OF TAHITI

and Cook wisely made friends with them. The weather was so warm on this island that the natives wore few clothes; usually only long strips of cloth wound round their bodies. The men covered themselves with tatooing; usually there were patterns of "men, birds or dogs". Their two favourite foods were coco-nuts and fish, and before eating them the natives carefully washed their hands, for they were very clean in their habits.

The Chief of Tahiti gave Cook permission to set up an observatory from which he could view the eclipse, and also to build huts for use during his stay on the island. On a clear, cloudless day, on June 3, 1769, Cook and his party observed the eclipse of the sun under perfect weather conditions. When their work was completed, Cook bade farewell to his friends on the lovely island of Tahiti, and sailed in a south-westerly direction till he sighted the islands which Tasman had discovered over a hundred and twenty-five years before. Cook found that the natives, the Maoris, were a "fierce, strong, raw-boned, well-made, active people, very dark brown in colour, with black hair, black beards and sparkling white teeth". So warlike were they that Cook had to warn his men to beware of going ashore without guards. Often the Maoris would paddle out to his ship in their canoes and call out, "Come here, come ashore with us and we will kill you." Although Cook wanted to land and get supplies of fresh fruit and vegetables, he dared not. To this place he gave the name Poverty Bay. At other places he made landings, but everywhere he found that the natives were very treacherous. He also made the unpleasant discovery that the Maoris were cannibals.

For over six months Cook sailed along the coasts of New Zealand for a distance of two thousand, four hundred miles, charting the bays, straits and capes, and giving them such names as Cape Farewell, Cape Turnagain and Cook Strait. After taking possession of New Zealand in the name of the King of England, he sailed westward.

Three weeks later he reached the unexplored eastern shore of Australia. Here in a little bay where he landed, he found many beautiful flowers and rare plants, and to this place he gave the name Botany Bay. On the trunk of a huge tree one of his men made carvings telling of Cook's arrival there and the name of his ship. Nine miles north of Botany Bay was a fine harbour which Cook named Port Jackson; to-day beside this great inlet stands the city of Sydney, the finest and most important seaport in all of Australia.

Continuing north Cook mapped the bays, islands and capes on his charts, and made many landings. The natives of Eastern Australia were, like the Maoris, a tall, dark people with long, black hair and they were equally savage. Again Cook was forced to warn his sailors not to venture too far from the ship lest the treacherous natives, who were expert with bows and arrows, should kill them.

The *Endeavour* had now reached very dangerous waters, for off the coast lay a wall of coral which is now known as the Great Barrier Reef. One clear, moonlit night, the *Endeavour* piled up on the reef and stuck fast. The only hope of getting her off was to lighten the ship, so over forty tons of precious cargo, guns, casks and stores were tossed overboard; still she remained fast on the reef. When the tide rose, however, the ship was freed again, but much damage had been done. The sharp-pointed coral had gashed a hole in the vessel's side and water was pouring into the hold. Cook and his men

SHE CARRIED HER YOUNG IN A LITTLE POUCH

were in a terrible plight, for the ship was over twenty miles from shore and was sinking fast. All hands manned the pumps and toiled to keep the ship from going down. At last the shore was reached. After the *Endeavour* was beached the great hole was repaired. To the place where the ship landed Cook gave the name Cape Tribulation and the near-by bay was named Cook Bay. Many strange mouse-coloured animals were seen in this land. These slender animals leapt or bounded with great speed over the ground. Their hind legs were very powerful. When one of them was shot and cooked for dinner the men were delighted with its fine flavour. These animals, now known as kangaroos, had many strange habits. The men noticed that the mother kangaroo carried her young in a little pouch or pocket, and when the young kangaroo got tired or when danger threatened, it hopped into her pouch for rest or protection.

The explorers had been away from home for over two years. Cook decided to return home. Before leaving the new land he took possession of the great island continent in the name of the King of England, and named it New South Wales. The *Endeavour* then sailed north and west, through a strait between New Guinea and Australia. Thus Cook proved that New Guinea was an island, separate from New South Wales (Australia).

A call was made at Java and then Cook sailed for England by way of the Indian Ocean and the Cape of Good Hope. He reached home after a journey around the world which had taken him three years. The king received Captain James Cook in St. James's Palace. The great navigator presented his sovereign with a journal of his long voyage, together with carefully-made maps and charts of the places he had visited.

Cook had been successful in carrying out all of the things he had planned to do. Naturally he felt pleased with his discoveries, but what pleased him most can best be told in his own words: "I have not lost one man by sickness during the whole voyage." Not one man had died of scurvy during a voyage of over sixty thousand miles. Cook had set a new record for health among his seamen.

SECOND VOYAGE

Within a year Cook sailed again to the South Seas. He was instructed, this time, to search for a great southern continent which was thought to exist far to the south of New South Wales (Australia). Little was known of this part of the world for, up until this time, no ship had ventured into these waters. Cook was ready to accept the challenge. After reaching the Cape of Good Hope his two ships, the *Resolution* and *Adventure,* headed south, crossed the Antarctic Circle and entered seas in which huge fields of ice lay on every side. Storms and gales swept the decks and the cold grew worse as the days passed. On one occasion a huge iceberg, almost a mile in length, was sighted. Cook's crew were the first men to see the marvellous display of multi-coloured lights, now called the Southern Lights, which resemble the Northern Lights of the Arctic. After sailing for one hundred and seventeen days through these dangerous seas and finding no land Cook sailed to New Zealand, where he and his crew rested.

Two more attempts were made to reach Antarctica, but each time the ships were forced back by great fields of ice. On all three attempts Cook failed to sight land, and he recorded that if any land was in this region it must be a frozen and desolate place and so far to the south that it would be of little or no value to man. On the way back Cook visited a strange barren island, Easter Island, where he found seven hundred enormous stone statues, several of which were over seventy feet in height. No one knows who carved or built these statues out of hard rock. To this day they remain a puzzle and a mystery. Another island which Cook discovered and took possession of, in the name of the King of England, was South Georgia, which lies far to the south-east of the tip of South America and is now an important whaling station.

After a journey of three years, which again had taken Captain Cook all the way around the world, he landed back in Plymouth, England. He returned to report that he was fully satisfied that there was no southern continent and that even if one did exist it would be of no help to man. Again

Cook was able to report that he had not lost a single man from scurvy.

THIRD VOYAGE

On Cook's next voyage, one year later, he planned to explore the Pacific Ocean, which lies between Asia and

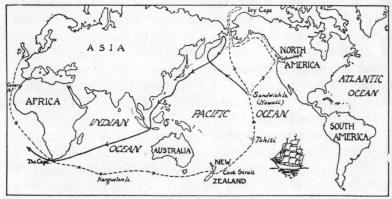

CAPTAIN COOK'S LAST VOYAGE

North America. He wondered if a water-passage could be found from the Pacific to the Atlantic to the north of America.

On the way to the Pacific calls were made at Tasmania, New Zealand and Tahiti. On December twenty-fifth the explorers rested at a pleasant little tropical island, and in honour of the occasion they named it Christmas Island. Here they found green turtles, three hundred of them, some of which they cooked and ate instead of the usual roast turkey. Many days later the ships approached a group of beautiful islands in the middle of the Pacific Ocean. Cook named them the Sandwich Islands in honour of one of his friends in England, the Earl of Sandwich. On Hawaii he found an active volcano, one of the largest in the world. The natives were a tall, strong, friendly people, who were good farmers and grew bananas, coco-nuts and yams, which are similar to sweet potatoes. Hawaiian homes were well built of wood, with thatched roofs made of palm leaves. The natives were thieves and from time to time the Englishmen found hammers, knives and other things missing, especially those made of metal. Cook also found that they were cannibals.

Heading in a north-easterly direction, the ships sailed on until they reached the western shores of North America. Near the mouth of the Columbia River they visited an Indian village, and there saw the copper-skinned straight-haired natives dressed in warm clothes made of fur, for the weather at this time was quite cold. Tall poles bearing the carved figures of birds, fish and animals greatly interested the Englishmen. These were totem poles. When the ships put out to sea again they were driven by strong winds far out from the shore, and after travelling for many days they reached a bleak fog-bound land which is known to-day as Alaska. Cook was searching for a passage to the east to the Atlantic Ocean, but the land seemed to be bending to the west. In a few days the ships reached a narrow strait and sailing through it Cook found himself in a great icy sea. Nowadays we know that he had passed through Bering Strait, which lies between Asia and North America, and had entered the Arctic Ocean. He had crossed the Arctic Circle and had reached great fields of ice-covered waters. Hundreds of huge walruses were seen sporting on the ice-cakes, some of which were killed and cooked. The sailors found their flesh rather tough, but at least it provided the crew with fresh meat. Because winter was approaching and because no passage could be found, but only a solid wall of ice over twelve feet in height, Cook decided to return to the Sandwich Islands and not risk the lives of his men further.

He planned to spend the winter in the Sandwich islands and in the spring to make another search for the passage. In the islands, however, the thieving habits of the natives led to a great deal of trouble between them and Cook's crew. On one occasion a large boat, a cutter, was stolen. Cook

went ashore to settle the trouble in a friendly but firm manner. He found the natives in an ugly mood. Suddenly one of them sprang upon Cook from behind and struck him with an iron dagger. The blow stunned Cook and he fell heavily to the ground. Before his men could help him the natives, armed with stone clubs, swarmed around him and beat him to death.

THE NATIVES BEAT HIM TO DEATH

Thus died Captain James Cook, great seaman and explorer. During his life-time he had done much for his king and his country. He had planted the British flag on the eastern coast of Australia; he had sailed around the entire coast of the two islands that make up New Zealand; and he had discovered many islands in many oceans. Cook had sailed further north into the Arctic Ocean and further south into the Antarctic than any other man.

His achievements as a seaman, a scientist and an explorer were great; but of equal importance to humanity, and perhaps Cook's greatest discovery, was a successful method of combating scurvy and thus saving lives.

TEST

Tell which word or phrase of the column on the right is closely associated with the words in the left-hand column:

COLUMN I	COLUMN II
1. The Island where Cook observed an eclipse of the sun.	(a) scurvy
2. A disease brought on by a lack of fresh fruits, vegetables and meats in the diet.	(b) Hawaiian
3. A mouse-coloured animal that Cook saw in Eastern Australia.	(c) totem poles
4. An island on which Cook found hundreds of huge stone statues.	(d) walrus
5. The name by which the Sandwich Islands are known to-day.	(e) Easter
6. A vegetable like our sweet potatoes which was grown on the Sandwich Islands.	(f) New South Wales
7. Great carved poles which Cook saw in the Indian villages in Western Canada.	(g) Tahiti
8. An animal which Cook saw in the Arctic Ocean.	(h) South Georgia
9. An island, discovered by Cook, which is now a whaling station.	(i) yams
10. Name which Cook gave to the continent of Australia.	(j) kangaroo

THINGS TO DO TOGETHER

1. Make an illustration using crayons showing Cook landing at Botany Bay.
2. Look up interesting information about: (a) the following animals of Australia: kangaroo, duck-billed platypus, koala bear; (b) the following birds of Australia: kookaburra, lyre bird.
3. On a map of the Pacific area mark Cook's route on his third and last voyage. Locate the following places on your map: Bering Sea, Sandwich Islands, Columbia River, Alaska, Christmas Island, New Zealand.

THINGS TO DO SEPARATELY

1. Make a collection of pictures of Hawaii, under the following headings: natives, beaches, palm-trees, homes and fruits.
2. What disaster occurred at Pearl Harbour in the Hawaiian Islands in December 1941?

BOOKS TO READ

FOR THE TEACHER

Great Navigators and Discoverers, J. A. Brendon. *Geo. G. Harrap & Co. Ltd.*

Exploration and Discovery, Arthur Archer. *Cambridge University Press.*

A Book of Seamen, F. H. Doughty. *Jonathan Cape.*

A History of Geographical Discovery & Exploration, J. N. L. Baker. *Geo. G. Harrap & Co. Ltd.*

FOR THE PUPIL

Heroes of Discovery, Robert Finch. *University of London Press.*

The Book of Discovery, T. C. Bridges. *Geo. Harrap & Co. Ltd.*

A Book of Discovery, M. B. Synge. *Thos. Nelson & Sons.*

Map Makers, Cottler and Jaffe. *The Ryerson Press.*

The Foundations of History, Book D, Phyllis Wragge. *Thos. Nelson & Sons.*

THE BUCCANEERS
HENRY MORGAN

One hundred years after Drake's raids on Spanish settlements in the West Indies, there appeared a group of rough, lawless men, mostly Englishmen, who roamed the waters of the Caribbean Sea, raiding Spanish towns both on the islands and on the Spanish Main. They made their headquarters on the island of Jamaica, which was owned by Britain, and from their secret base they launched attacks on the Spaniards, seizing their ships and carrying away rich treasures of gold and silver. These pirates were also known as boucan-eaters or buccaneers, because of a meat which they prepared and ate, called boucan. It was a dried beef and it kept in good condition during their long voyages at sea.

Perhaps the best known of the buccaneers was an Englishman, Henry Morgan. As a youth he had gone to the island of Barbadoes to work on a sugar plantation; but growing tired of the quiet life there, he had joined a pirate band and journeyed to its camp in Jamaica. Because of his courage, charm and leadership, it was not long before he was in command of the pirate band.

The governor of Jamaica knew that this pirate hideaway was not far from the British town, but he did little to stop their attacks on the Spaniards. In fact he felt that the buccaneers afforded the best defence of his island against the Spaniards.

After Morgan became leader, he led many successful attacks on Spanish galleons and Spanish towns. One of his most daring raids was on the town of Porto Bello on the Spanish Main. It was from this place that much gold and silver was shipped overseas to Spain. For many weeks beforehand, Morgan made careful plans for the attack. He set his men to work sharpening cutlasses and packing supplies into sturdy sea-chests. He himself pored over maps and made plans. When all was ready, Morgan and his band sailed, with the greatest of secrecy, from Jamaica, and landed in a little cove three miles from Porto Bello. Making their way through the tropical forests, they reached the Spanish town and took it completely by surprise. From its rich warehouses they seized a fortune in gold and silver, over one hundred thousand pieces of eight. Spaniards who refused to give up their gold and jewels were tortured cruelly until they told of the hiding-places of their treasures.

Morgan's success on this adventure encouraged him to make plans for a greater raid, this time on Panama, the

DANGERS LURKED IN THE TROPICAL JUNGLES

richest of the Spanish towns. Panama was on the west coast of the Isthmus of Panama and to this town came the richly-laden Spanish galleons from Chile and Peru. Here their treasures were unloaded from the ships and reloaded to be sent overland by mule trains to Porto Bello and then, by ship, to Spain.

With a band of sixteen hundred men, Morgan sailed from Jamaica and landed near Porto Bello, but this time the Spaniards were ready for him and a fierce battle took place. Although the buccaneers won, they paid dearly for their victory, for nearly half of their number was either killed or wounded. Undaunted by this piece of bad luck,

Morgan led his remaining men across the narrow Isthmus of Panama, which joins North and South America. With them they took little food, for they hoped to seize whatever they needed from the Spanish settlements along the way. Unfortunately for Morgan, many of the towns had been warned of his coming, and the Spaniards had fled into hiding places, leaving behind few supplies. Morgan's food supplies grew less and less; nowhere could he find anything to eat. In desperation his men ate the leather from their clothing and the harness from the donkeys and mules. More hardships lay ahead. They were attacked by fierce Indians, who hid in the trees and shot poisoned arrows from overhead on the unlucky buccaneers. Fierce alligators, lurking along the river bank, sometimes seized not-too-watchful pirates in their mighty jaws. Dangers lurked in the tropical jungles too, for many of the men fell ill with yellow fever and malaria. At all times the heat was almost unbearable. After journeying for six days in those conditions many of Morgan's men begged their leader to give up his wild scheme and return to Jamaica. Henry Morgan, great leader that he was, calmed their fears and assured them that their troubles would soon be over. Next day a miracle seemed to happen, for they came upon a barn well filled with grain. So great was the hunger of the men that they seized handfuls of the grain and ate it raw and and dry.

On the ninth day of their march the weary buccaneers reached their goal, the town of Panama. The Spaniards were wholly unprepared for an attack from the land side, and all their guns were pointed out to sea. The Spaniards drove a herd of wild bulls into Morgan's band, hoping to put the buccaneers to flight. However, Morgan commanded his men to fire on the excited bulls and the animals in wild disorder wheeled around and rushed amongst the Spaniards, trampling and killing many of them. In the confusion that followed Panama fell to Morgan. The joy of the buccaneers knew no bounds and they planned a great celebration. Again Morgan showed himself a wise leader. He feared that, while his men were celebrating the victory, the Spaniards might reorganize and re-take the town, so he told his men that all the wine in Panama was poisoned and that they were not to touch a drop of it. For three weeks Morgan made his men rest. Then they set to work to gather in the plunder. A vast store of treasure was collected, enough for two hundred mule loads; the city itself was set on fire and the victorious men returned overland, taking the treasures with them. Morgan had overcome the greatest of difficulties and had carried out an exploit that even Drake had not been able to accomplish. With only a small band of starving, weary men, he had seized the mightiest Spanish stronghold in the New World.

Morgan had stirred up much trouble, however. Spain was furious with Britain for allowing a band of British buccaneers to attack Spanish towns in the New World. When Morgan returned to Jamaica he was arrested and sent by ship to England, to be tried for piracy. However, when this handsome buccaneer arrived in London, he so charmed the hearts of all the people he met that he not only was given his freedom, but he received a knighthood from King Charles I. Soon he returned to Jamaica as governor of the island.

Sir Henry Morgan, Governor of Jamaica, was a very different man from Henry Morgan the pirate. He became a model governor. He dressed in the finest of clothes. He wore brocade coats and velvet breeches; had buttons of pure silver and ruffles of the finest lace. Proudly he carried about with him a treasured silver snuff box, the gift of King Charles I of England. To their sorrow he would have nothing to do with his former pirate friends. Indeed he banished them from the waters of the West Indies. Many of them scattered to distant places, the west coast of South America, the islands of the Pacific, and even to far-off Australia.

TEST

Write an answer to each of the following questions.

1. Where was the pirate headquarters in the West Indies?
2. By what other name were the pirates known?
3. Why did Morgan attack the town of Porto Bello on the Spanish Main?
4. Why was Morgan's attack on Panama considered to be his greatest and most famous raid?
5. What were two of the hardships Morgan and his men endured on the way to this Spanish town?
6. What means did the men of Panama use to defend their city?
7. Why did Morgan tell his men that all the wine in Panama was poisoned?
8. After the raid on Panama, why was Morgan taken to London, England?
9. What did the King of England, Charles I, do for Henry Morgan?
10. When Morgan returned to Jamaica, how did he treat his former friends?

THINGS TO DO TOGETHER

1. What are Jamaica's chief exports?
2. Make an illustration showing a pirate standing on the deck of his ship. This pirate has one leg and is blind in one eye.

THINGS TO DO SEPARATELY

1. Find out how you would probably travel across the Isthmus of Panama to-day.

2. Read Robert Louis Stevenson's book, *Treasure Island*.
3. What did the pirates mean when they used the following words: pieces of eight, the black spot, a pirate's mate, the Jolly Roger, bullion?
4. Collect pictures of famous pirates and put them on display on the bulletin board.

BOOKS TO READ

FOR THE TEACHER
Great Navigators and Discoverers, J. A. Brendon. *Geo. G. Harrap & Co. Ltd.*

FOR THE PUPIL
A Book of Famous Pirates, A. M. Smyth. *Oxford University Press.*
Book of Pirates, Howard Pyle. *Harper & Brothers.*

WILLIAM DAMPIER

When the pirates were driven by Sir Henry Morgan from the West Indies, many sailed to the west coast of South America, hoping to continue raiding Spanish ships and towns there. However, the great Spanish galleons were fewer in number now than they had been in former times, and those at sea were well-armed and ready to fight. Most of the Spanish towns were well fortified too, and able to put up a stiff fight against unfriendly ships entering the harbours.

Several ships decided to leave these unprofitable shores and head west across the Pacific Ocean in search of riches and adventure. Amongst these was the *Cygnet,* commanded by Captain Swan, with William Dampier as sailing-master. No Englishman for many years had sailed on a voyage such as this, and every member of the crew was filled with excitement, hoping for the riches they had been told abounded in the East Indies and the islands of the Great South Sea.

As day after day passed and no land came in sight, the crew grew discontented. Their supplies of food had grown smaller and smaller, and after fifty days at sea they were faced with death by starvation. They began to eye each other and several of them murmured that, when all the food was gone, they would break their fast by eating Captain Swan, who was a plump, robust fellow. When poor Swan heard of these rumours he said to Dampier, "Ah Dampier! you are lucky that you are so bony and thin, for you would make a poor meal for my men, and none of them will think of eating you!" Luckily for Swan, land was sighted, and before long the buccaneers landed on the Ladrone Islands to the south-east of Asia, where the hungry men broke their fast on coco-nuts, fruit and rice.

The crew had given Swan much trouble on the long journey. They had openly declared that they were dissatisfied with him as their leader for, they vowed, he had nearly led them to death by starvation. It was agreed that Swan was to be left behind on the islands, and the *Cygnet* sailed south with another captain, William Dampier. After many days at sea the ship reached a new coast. It was New Holland, which we now know as Australia. Fresh water aboard the ship was running low, and men were sent in search of a supply. No streams or springs were found along the barren, dry, sandy shores of this new land. Few animals or birds of any kind were to be seen, and of the natives Dampier wrote in his diary, "They are the miserablest people in the world." Indeed they did prove to be a very backward people. They lived in the open air, their only shelter being a piece of the bark of a tree, for they could not build huts of any kind. Their only clothing was a piece of bark wrapped around their waists, in the form of a clumsy skirt. Fish was their only food. Because they had never discovered how to make hooks or lines, they caught the fish in their hands in the little pools of salt water which formed along the sands. When they caught no fish

"THE MISERABLEST PEOPLE IN THE WORLD"

they went hungry. The backward manner of living of these dark-skinned fuzzy-haired Bushmen of Australia discouraged Dampier. He left the country and sailed northward again.

The ship's crew behaved no better with Dampier than it had with Captain Swan. Dampier decided to leave this "mad crew," as he called them, at the next place his ship called. This was Nicobar Island. With three others from the ship he set out, in a frail canoe, for the island of Sumatra, from which he hoped to go by ship back home to Britain. Thus was begun one of the most daring voyages ever attempted by a white man. The distance between the two islands was over one hundred and twenty miles, and twice during the voyage the canoe upset. Supplies, charts and men were thrown into the sea. Somehow, after five days amidst heavy seas and severe storms, the canoe arrived safely in Sumatra.

Many months later Dampier reached England. He was penniless. He had brought back none of the riches he had hoped to find, but he had with him an unhappy black native from one of the islands of the East Indies. He hoped to put this "Prince Jeoly," as he named him, on show to the curious British and thus make some money. Unfortunately for Dampier, the "Prince" fell ill with smallpox, and died soon after he reached England. Dampier had also brought home a long piece of bamboo, waxed at both ends, which contained his diary and an account of all his travels. Little had escaped his observant eye. From these notes Dampier wrote a book telling the story of his long voyages. People who read it were delighted with the stories of his strange adventures. When it reached the hands of the King of England he was so interested that he invited Dampier to the palace and told him of his desire to send an expedition to New Holland. No better man, he said, could be found to lead this expedition than William Dampier.

Dampier willingly accepted the offer. In the *Roebuck* he started out to learn more of the land, its people and its minerals. Although he planned to sail by way of Cape Horn across the Pacific Ocean to New Holland, winds drove his vessel around the Cape of Good Hope, and Dampier reached the west shore of that continent. At first the shores were bleak and barren, but further north they proved more inviting. At one place he found sweet-scented trees, rich soil and curious animals, stranger than any that Dampier had ever before seen. One of these "a sort of raccoon, with short fore-legs and great jumping hind legs" was the kangaroo, now the emblem of Australia. In the bay the sailors caught a great many sharks, which provided the crew with fresh meat. These sharks must have been of great size, for in the stomach of one was found the head and bones of a hippopotamus. Dampier appropriately named this place Shark's Bay.

Drinking water was running low, and as no fresh water could be found, the men sailed north along the coast in search of it. None was found. After a journey of over nine hundred miles they reached the pleasant island of Timor, where they found plenty of drinking water and fresh fruit.

On this journey Dampier made splendid maps of all the places he had visited in New Holland, Timor, New Guinea and New Britain. Dampier's voyage resulted in the first real mapping of lands which until this time were little known by the people of Europe.

Because the stormy season was drawing on and because the *Roebuck* was not seaworthy, Dampier decided to return to England to tell of his discoveries, and to ask the king to give him a better ship in which to explore further along the coasts of the new regions. As the vessel crossed the Indian Ocean and rounded the Cape of Good Hope, Dampier's fears for the ship grew, for water oozed through leaks in the rotten sides of the ship. The pumps were put into use and went both day and night. By the time the ship reached mid-Atlantic all hope for her was gone. Luckily the *Roebuck* was not far from the tiny island of Ascension. Just within sight of shore the vessel sank. A raft was hastily made, on which the survivors loaded a few stores and made for shore.

Ascension is merely a rock jutting up out of the great

ocean. Few ships ever call there. For five weeks the weary, hungry ship-wrecked sailors waited in vain for a ship to rescue them. Finally one came. They were taken back to England, where they were bitterly disappointed by the cool welcome that they received. Poor Dampier suffered more than the others. Where was the gold that he was to have brought back? How had he lost his ship? Questions of this kind were asked him. Few people even bothered to glance at the excellent maps and accounts of his journey that he had managed to bring safely back to England. He was tried by court-martial and was found "not a fit person to be employed as commander of any of His Majesty's ships".

Dampier, great explorer and buccaneer that he was, received little honour for his work. He had sailed on long, dangerous voyages and he had visited distant lands, but he had lacked one important quality, good leadership. The most important result of his voyages was the production of the excellent maps and good accounts of the lands he had visited and the seas on which he had sailed. These were to provide a mine of information and encouragement for the many explorers who were to follow him.

TEST

Fill in the blank spaces with suitable words.

1. Dampier and Swan sailed to the islands of the Great South Sea to find ———— and ————.
2. Their journey across the Pacific Ocean took over ———— days.
3. The crew grew so hungry that they said that they would eat ————.
4. However, they finally reached the ———— Islands where they were given plenty of food.
5. Dampier declared that the "miserablest" people in all the world lived in ————.

6. On one occasion he made a daring voyage of over a hundred miles from Nicobar Island to Sumatra in a —————.
7. All of Dampier's maps and his diary were carried in a ————— —————.
8. When Dampier returned to Australia on a second voyage he saw a strange animal called a —————.
9. Returning home from his second voyage, Dampier's ship was wrecked off the coast of ————— Island in mid-Atlantic.
10. When he arrived in England he was questioned because he had lost his ship and had brought no ————— back with him.

THINGS TO DO TOGETHER

1. On a map of the world, trace in the route taken by Dampier on his first voyage. Use green crayon for this route. Trace in the route taken on the second voyage using red crayon. On your map locate the following places: Ladrone Islands, New Holland, Nicobar Island, Shark's Bay, Ascension Island, England.
2. Make a picture of Australia and show the products that are found there.
3. Make a sketch showing Dampier arriving on the island of Sumatra after a journey over the seas from Nicobar Island.

THINGS TO DO SEPARATELY

1. Find pictures of the natives of Australia.
2. Why was the island of Ascension of great importance to the Allied Air Force in the Second World War?

BOOKS TO READ

FOR THE TEACHER

Great Navigators and Discoverers, J. A. Brendon. *Geo. G. Harrap & Co. Ltd.*

Exploration and Discovery, Arthur Archer. *Cambridge University Press.*

FOR THE PUPIL

A Book of Discovery, M. B. Synge. *Thos. Nelson & Sons.*

ALEXANDER SELKIRK

One year after Dampier returned from his disastrous voyage to the South Seas, a fleet of ships manned by English buccaneers sailed from the shores of Britain to prey on French and Spanish ships off the west coast of South America. The commander of the fleet was Captain Thomas Stradling. On this expedition William Dampier was no longer in an important position; he was sailing-master aboard one of the smaller ships.

After spending many months on the ocean, the seamen ran short of fresh water and meat. They made their way to the islands of Juan Fernandez which lie off the coast of Chile, where they knew that they could obtain fresh supplies. This tiny group of islands is difficult to reach, for along the coast there are rocks and there are also treacherous currents near the shore. The buccaneers were excellent seamen and a safe landing was made on one of the islands. When the supplies were obtained, the pirates prepared to leave the island. In the meantime, trouble had arisen between the captain of one of the ships and a crew member on his vessel. The trouble-maker was Alexander Selkirk, a native of Scotland, who complained about the leaky condition of the ship. He said he would not sail until the ship was repaired. The complaint reached the ears of the commander, Captain Stradling, who decided to maroon Selkirk on the lonely uninhabited island of Juan Fernandez as punishment for the trouble he had caused.

At first Selkirk did not mind his lot, for he enjoyed roaming through the lovely valleys and climbing the green hills. The weather was warm and the days were long and sunny. The buccaneers had left him some supplies, clothing, bedding, a gun, a pound of powder, tobacco, an axe, a knife, a kettle, and some books, one of which was the Bible. Selkirk hoped that in a few weeks some ship would call at the island and that before long he would return home to Britain.

Days passed, but no ship came near the island. Selkirk decided to make some kind of shelter to protect himself from wind and rain. He built two huts, one a cook-house and the other a reading-room and bedroom. The walls of each hut were made from the wood of a tree which grew on the island, the pimento tree, and the conical roofs were covered with long grass. The skins of goats lined the huts and kept out draughts.

His main food was the flesh of goats. These animals were found in great numbers roaming over the island. During his stay on the island Selkirk killed over five hundred goats for food. More than anything else, Selkirk missed bread and salt. Two vegetables which grew in quantities on the island were turnips and cabbage. The turnips had, years before, been planted by Dampier's men when they had visited the island and, in the meantime, they had overspread acres of ground.

Selkirk was surprised to find great numbers of cats and rats on Juan Fernandez. These animals had stolen ashore from ships which had called at the islands for food, wood and water. The rats proved to be a great nuisance for they ate his precious store of food and clothing and they even gnawed his toes while he slept. He pampered and petted the cats, feeding them on goat's flesh till they became tame and fond of him. His friends, the cats, attacked the rats and in time he was rid of the troublemakers.

Before long Selkirk's clothing and shoes wore out and he was forced to make himself coat, cape, and hat of goatskins. Instead of thread he used thin strips of goat-skin and a clumsy needle was made from a nail sharpened on the stones. Selkirk did without shoes, for his feet had become hard from running over the rocks and he was able to go about barefoot.

As days, weeks, and months passed with no sign of a ship, Selkirk grew very lonely. Each day he scanned the horizon for signs of a sail. During his long stay on the island only two ships came to anchor there but unfortunate-

FOUR YEARS PASSED SLOWLY BY

ly both of them were Spanish ships of war. In terror, Selkirk hid in a tree, for he chose rather to die alone on the island than to fall into the hands of the enemy Spaniards who would have murdered him or forced him to work as a slave in the silver mines in South America.

Four years slowly passed by. Selkirk had almost given up hope of ever again seeing the shores of his native land. Then one morning he sighted the dim outline of a fleet of ships far out at sea. Nearer and nearer they came to the island. As they approached the shore, Selkirk was over-joyed to find that they were flying the flag of Britain.

The commander of the ships was a Captain Woodes-Rogers and the ships were manned by buccaneers bent on plundering Spanish towns and attacking Spanish ships. On landing, Captain Woodes-Rogers was astonished to find, on the shore to greet him, a strange wild-looking man clothed in the skins of goats. Selkirk was unable to speak, for in the past four years he had talked to no one and had lost the power of speech. When he regained his voice he related to the astonished seamen the story of his lonely life on the island. One of the men who was particularly surprised to see Selkirk was William Dampier. He was sure Selkirk had perished.

Selkirk signed on as mate on one of the ships and the fleet sailed out into the blue waters of the Pacific. During their travels the pirates attacked not only a great Spanish treasure galleon richly laden with gold and silver but also fourteen other Spanish ships. When they returned to Britain after a journey which took them round the world, they unloaded spoil which was valued at two hundred thousand pounds. Alexander Selkirk received his share of the riches.

Selkirk caused great excitement in London. The story of his long stay on the uninhabited island of Juan Fernandez became the talk of the town. Wherever he appeared people crowded around to catch a glimpse of him. Captain Woodes-Rogers wrote a book telling of his voyage around the world and of the rescue of Alexander Selkirk from the lonely isle. This book fell into the hands of Daniel Defoe, a writer, and the story of Selkirk inspired him to write the famous novel, *Robinson Crusoe*. It is quite true that Defoe chose a different name for the hero of his book and he also chose the island of Tobago, off the north-eastern coast of South America, as the setting for his story, but for the most part the two stories are similar.

Alexander Selkirk, after a short visit to his old home in Largo, Fife County, Scotland, returned to London. He married and lived there for the rest of his life, never again venturing to far-off places.

TEST

Choose the word or words that will make the statement correct:

1. Selkirk was cast ashore on the lonely island of
> South Georgia
> Juan Fernandez
> Tierra del Fuego

2. The island is
> south-east of South America
> west of South America
> to the south of South America

3. Selkirk remained there for over
> four years
> ten years
> twenty years

4. His food was for the most part the flesh of
> goats
> cows
> horses

5. What he missed more than any other food was
> sugar
> salt
> pepper

6. When his clothing wore out, he made new outfits from
> the skins of rats
> the skins of goats
> dried palm leaves

7. When some Spanish seamen visited the island, Selkirk
> hid from them
> fired on them
> refused to go with them to Peru

8. The British captain who rescued him from the island was
   William Dampier
   Captain Woodes-Rogers
   Captain Thomas Stradling
9. The Englishman who wrote the story of Selkirk's life on the uninhabited island was
   William Shakespeare
   Daniel Defoe
   Robert Louis Stevenson
10. After his return to Britain from his exile, Selkirk spent the rest of his life
   sailing to far-off places
   in Britain
   in the West Indies

THINGS TO DO TOGETHER

1. Several pupils in the class should obtain children's copies of the book *Robinson Crusoe* from the nearest library and after reading the story tell the most interesting parts to the other members of the class.
2. On a large blackboard map of the world, mark in the route Selkirk took in going from Britain to the uninhabited island where he was marooned. Mark in the route that the ships which rescued him took on their return to Britain.
3. Draw in colour a picture of Robinson Crusoe one year after he was stranded on the island. In the background show his home and the trees you would find growing there.

THINGS TO DO SEPARATELY

1. Pretend that you have been cast ashore on a far-off island. On which island would you like to land? Why?
2. Imagine that you are Robinson Crusoe. What might you have written in your diary (*a*) on the night you were marooned on the island, (*b*) one year later, (*c*) on the night of your rescue, (*d*) the night you returned to Britain?

3. These lines are part of a well-known poem written by William Cowper and telling of Alexander Selkirk's stay on the lonely island. Memorize these famous lines.

> I am monarch of all I survey
> My right there is none to dispute,
> From the centre all round to the sea,
> I am lord of the fowl and the brute.
> O solitude! where are the charms
> That sages have seen in thy face?
> Better dwell in the midst of alarms,
> Than reign in this horrible place.

BOOKS TO READ

FOR THE TEACHER

Commodore Anson's Voyage into the South Seas and Around the World, Vice-Admiral Boyle Sommerville. *William Heinemann Ltd.*

A Cruising Voyage Round the World, Captain Woodes-Rogers. *Cassell & Co., Ltd.*

Great Navigators and Discoverers, J. A. Brendon. *George G. Harrap & Co. Ltd.*

FOR THE PUPIL

The Book of Discovery, T. C. Bridges. *George G. Harrap & Co. Ltd.*

HERDS OF MILK-WHITE CATTLE

V. LIGHT ON THE DARK CONTINENT

BRUCE

FOR hundreds of years, men had sailed along the coasts of Africa but only a few had dared to explore very far inland. The Dark Continent and Africa the Unknown were names commonly given to this land of mystery. Men had travelled up the great river Nile but none had reached its source. Some map-makers said that it rose in the Mountains of the Moon, others that it sprang up somewhere in the great Sahara Desert. Of those few who had ventured far up the river, some never returned and those who did had failed to find its source. In those days, the dangers for a traveller in Northern Africa were many. The hot sun, the wild animals and fierce warlike tribes were only a few of the many difficulties facing those brave men who sought the source of the mighty river.

A tall young Scotsman, James Bruce, believed that the land of Abyssinia held the secret of the Nile's source and he was determined to seek it there.   In his diary he wrote, "I am resolved that this great discovery shall either be achieved by me or remain as it has done for thousands of years a defiance to all travellers."   He had prepared himself for this journey in many ways.   In Scotland Bruce had spent two years studying Oriental languages; he had also studied medicine.   He had made many journeys in North Africa, Greece and the Holy Land.   When the British government appointed him to a position in North Africa, Bruce made trips inland and learned much of the Arabs and their language.

In 1768, Bruce felt he was ready to start on a journey up the Nile to find its source.   When he arrived in Cairo, he gained the friendship of the Bey, the ruler of Egypt.   The latter gave him valuable letters of introduction to all princes, kings and chieftains whose lands he might visit, asking them to treat Bruce well and give him help. Boarding a river boat, he began his trip upstream.   Past the pyramids and Sphinx his boat travelled till it came to the ruins of the once mighty cities of Luxor, Thebes and Karnak.   At a nearby Arab encampment, a Sheikh known as Nimmer the Tiger had fallen ill.   Bruce with his medical knowledge relieved the sick man's pain and in return Nimmer confided that he believed that the Nile rose far up in the mountains of Abyssinia. He added that to continue up the river would be suicide for Bruce.   The Shiekh's advice was to strike out across the desert to the Red Sea, sail to Abyssinia and then journey inland.

Joining a caravan, Bruce crossed the desolate Nubian desert where no tree, shrub or beast was to be seen. He tells us in his diary that "there are not even traces of any living creatures neither serpent nor lizard, antelope nor ostrich—

the usual inhabitants of the most dreary deserts." After a week's journey, the little mud-walled village of Kosseir on the Red Sea was reached. For safety's sake, Bruce disguised himself as a Turk and travelled by ship through the Red Sea to Massawa, the seaport and gateway to Abyssinia. Here the ruler received him with black looks, even when Bruce showed letters from the Bey and Nimmer the Tiger. However, when messengers from the King of Abyssinia came, asking that Doctor Bruce proceed at once to the capital city, the ruler in Massawa showed a more friendly manner.

The ninety-five day journey from the seaport to the capital city was so difficult that only a man with good health and an iron will could have stood such an ordeal. Bruce travelled through deep gorges and along difficult paths till he came to a high plateau. Here he saw great herds of milk-white cattle with long horns and silky hair grazing on the green slopes. He learned that the natives found the soil so fertile that crops of wheat, barley and peas were harvested three times a year. After passing a range of mountains whose peaks were buried in the clouds, Bruce arrived in the capital city which stood on a high hill and contained the clay huts of ten thousand families.

A terrible epidemic of small-pox was raging throughout the city; rich and poor alike were dying. Even the royal children were ill. Bruce arrived at the very moment when he was needed. The king begged him to help the suffering people. Bruce used only the simplest of remedies. He opened all of the doors and windows, and washed the patients with water and vinegar. In a few days many of the sick recovered. Bruce was in such high favour in the city that he was appointed governor of a province, a position he declined to take, transferring it to a friend.

A few weeks later, he set out on his journey to find the source of the Nile. He reached Lake Tsana through which the Nile flowed. Here he met a fierce native chief, Fasil, who told Bruce that the journey to the Nile's source would take at least a year. Fasil also tried to frighten Bruce by telling him that savage warriors would eat him. When Fasil saw that none of these things discouraged Bruce, he gave him a fine grey horse and seven rough-looking fellows as guards. "These fellows," said Fasil, "are all chiefs. With them, you may go through our country, as if it were your own. No man will hurt you." As each day passed travelling became more difficult for the explorer. Tropical rains drenched his clothes and countless insects bit and stung him until he could hardly stand the pain. Foot-sore and weary, Bruce at

BRUCE'S JOURNEY IN SEARCH OF THE SOURCE OF THE NILE

last came to a place where the Nile was only a shallow stream less that eighty yards in width. The natives warned him that the Nile was sacred to them and that he must remove his shoes before crossing the stream. For many days he journeyed upstream. Now the river banks were only six yards apart and as Bruce reached the source of the river his excitement grew to fever pitch. When Bruce reached the place where a tiny spring of water bubbled up from the soft green grass, he penned these words, "I have reached the source of the Nile on November 4, 1770; I stood on the spot which had baffled men for three thousand years. Though a mere private Briton I triumphed here in my own mind over kings and their armies." Bruce did not forget to thank God for his protection through many dangers and for bringing success to his expedition. Then, stooping down, he filled a coco-nut shell with Nile water and drank the health of His Majesty, George III of England.

Bruce was in error. He had not found the source of the Nile, but the source of the Blue Nile, which is a large tributary to the main river. It was left to other explorers to find the source of the main stream, the White Nile.

Bruce decided to trace the river down to the Mediterranean Sea. In crossing the Nubian desert, he suffered from the extreme heat, the choking sand and hostile attacks by the natives. After many strange adventures, he arrived in Cairo and from there journeyed to England. He arrived home in 1773, after a journey which had taken almost ten years.

The tale he told to the king and the people of England was so strange that many refused to believe that Bruce had ever been to Abyssinia. Others were interested and formed a society, the African Association, with the purpose of gathering funds for further exploration into this vast unknown continent.

Bruce had done much to arouse interest in African exploration. His diary is a fine record not only of the journey but of the climate of Abyssinia and of the life and customs of the people there.

TEST

Fill in the blanks with suitable words.

1. Bruce went to Africa to try to find the source of the ———— River.
2. Bruce believed that this river rose in the land of ————.
3. Bruce won the friendship of many of the natives because he was a ————.
4. After enduring many ———— he finally reached the source of the river.
5. He first gave thanks to God and then he drank a toast to King George III of England in a ———— ————.
6. Bruce had not found the source of the main stream of the great river but he had found a tributary which is now known as the ———— ————.
7. On his return, Bruce again visited the city of ———— which is the capital of Egypt.
8. When Bruce returned home, and told his story, many people became interested in ———— in Africa.

THINGS TO DO TOGETHER

1. Topics for Class Discussion:
   (*a*) How does the River Nile help the Egyptian people?
   (*b*) Why is it difficult to travel through Abyssinia, even to-day?
   (*c*) Why did the kings of Egypt build the Pyramids?
2. On a map of Africa locate the following places: Nile River, Mediterranean Sea, Cairo, Red Sea, Massawa, Abyssinia, Sahara Desert.

THINGS TO DO SEPARATELY

1. Bruce journeyed near the great Sahara Desert. Find out where there are other great deserts in the world. Write down the names of at least three of these deserts.
2. Cut out and paste into your Social Studies Scrap Book any pictures you can find of the Nile River, the Sphinx, and the Pyramids.

Mungo Park

In 1795, Mungo Park, a young Scottish doctor, was sent out by the African Society of Britain to explore the giant Niger River in West Africa and to visit the cities on its banks. Several men had already been sent out to trace the course of this mighty river. None had succeeded and some had died in the attempt. Park was determined to succeed where the others had failed.

He sailed for Africa on June 21st, and arrived at the little town of Jellifree on the banks of the Gambia river. He set to work to learn Mandingo, the language spoken by the West African negroes. At this port he watched helpless slaves being shipped to the West Indies to work on sugar plantations. In addition to this human cargo, quantities of gold and ivory were loaded on ships bound for ports in Europe.

When his preparations had been made, Park set out on his trip east. He was accompanied by two slave dealers, two trusted negro servants, Johnson and Demba, and by two other negroes. Park rode on horseback, the negroes had donkeys or walked. Their supplies included a change of clothing, quantities of food, beads, amber, tobacco, some pistols as well as an umbrella, a sextant, a thermometer and a compass.

Dangers lurked everywhere. Alligators and hippopotami hid in the deep muddy mangrove swamps along the river banks, and poisonous snakes lay coiled in the branches of the trees overhead ready to pounce down on the travellers.

In one village which the party visited, Park was given a feast by the black monarch to whom he presented his immense umbrella. Because this was a very important occasion, Park had worn his best coat with bright brass buttons. The king was so delighted with the coat that he persuaded the traveller to hand it over to him. The ladies of the court were filled with curiosity when they learned that Park's skin was all pure white. They vowed that his mother must have dipped him into milk every day when he was a baby.

MUNGO PARK GAZED ON THE MAJESTIC NIGER

The explorer made his way from village to village. Some natives were friendly and gave help to the weary travellers; more often Park met with unfriendly looks. In some villages part of his precious supplies was stolen, for the natives were expert thieves. On the whole, the negroes were kind and helpful but the Arab traders who hated the Christians tried to hinder his journey. A mighty Arab chief, Ali, treated Park brutally and imprisoned him in a hut with a pig as his only companion. This was the greatest insult an Arab could think of for a Christian. The women of the village were so inquisitive that they came in droves to stare at this strange white man and they even counted his fingers and toes to see if he had the same number as they had. The only person who showed him any kindness was Fatima, the chief's wife, who gave Park food and better living quarters. She also secretly helped him to escape into the neighbouring jungle. Here his horse and faithful little servant, Demba, were waiting for him.

Park had left the Gambia River and had travelled through jungles and swamps. At last he found himself on the banks of a great river which flowed to the eastward. This he felt certain was the Niger for which he had so long searched. All the hardships of the journey were forgotten as he gazed on the majestic river.

Nearby, Park found a town, the biggest he had yet seen, where he hoped to obtain food and supplies; but the people there refused to give him any help. At last an old woman took pity on him and led him to her hut where she gave him broiled fish to eat and shelter for the night. Next morning, in return for her kindness, Park gave her two of his precious brass buttons. On her advice he sent the King of Sego a gift of five thousand small shells, which pass as coins in that part of Africa, and he was allowed to enter the town. Here he was surprised to see solidly built clay houses, two stories in height. He learned from the King of Sego of a great city further down the river called Timbuctoo, a city of great wealth, where merchants from far-off places came to trade in slaves, gold and ivory.

As he pressed on, hoping to reach this mysterious city, he encountered more and more difficulties. Mosquitoes stung him and Park fell ill with malaria which is one of the great enemies of white men in tropical lands. He lay in the heart of the jungle five hundred miles from any European settlement. He had only the clothes he lay in, a ragged pair of breeches, a shirt and a tattered pair of shoes.

He still had his hat which shaded his head from the sun and in whose crown were all of his precious notes and drawings. His last friends, Demba and his horse, had died and he was all alone.

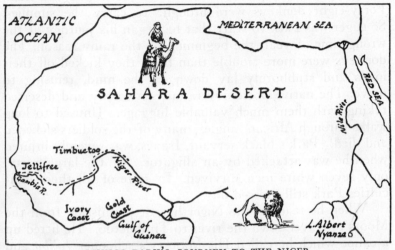

MUNGO PARK'S JOURNEY TO THE NIGER

If he continued his journey, he knew that he would die. Wisely, Park decided to turn back and, if possible, to get to the coast. He fell in with a caravan of slave dealers who made him promise in return for help, that they would be well paid for their trouble when the party reached Jellifree. Nine months later, worn out and ill, Park reached his friends who had thought they would never see him again. He joined a vessel leaving for England and arrived there after a journey which had taken two years and seven months.

Park married and settled down as a doctor in Scotland; but his heart was in Africa. He longed to find out more about Timbuctoo and to journey down the Niger to its mouth. In 1805, he was again sent out to Africa, this time by the British government. His party was made up of four Englishmen and an escort of forty-four British soldiers who proved to be quite unsuited for a journey of this kind. Forty-eight donkeys were brought to carry the supplies. So eager was Park to start that he began his journey at the wrong time of year, the beginning of the rainy season. The donkeys were more trouble than help, they kicked off their loads and stubbornly lay down in the mud, refusing to move. The native porters were untrustworthy and deserted taking with them much valuable luggage. Unused to long walks through African jungles, many of the soldiers sickened and died. Park's black servant, Isaacs, was severely injured when he was attacked by an alligator. Of the large party, only seven white men survived. In spite of all these difficulties Park still pressed on.

When he reached the Niger he got permission from the Moors to travel down the river to Timbuctoo. He fitted up a canoe which he called His Majesty's schooner *Joliba* and started down the broad river. Isaacs, his servant, was sent back to the coast with letters to Park's wife and friends and his diary telling of the progress he had made.

No word was received from Park for five years. At the end of that time Isaacs was chosen to head a search party to find any trace he could of his master. He learned from a native guide that Park had been attacked several times by unfriendly tribes. It was reported by natives that they had seen Park in the *Joliba* entering some rapids further down the river. His canoe had struck a rock and he had drowned.

Interest in Africa did not die with Park. Others carried on his work. Two Englishmen named Lander, twenty years later, journeyed down the Niger to its mouth and found it emptied its waters into the Atlantic.

TEST

Choose the word or words that will make each statement correct.

1. The Niger River is in
   - (a) West Africa
   - (b) South Africa
   - (c) East Africa.

2. On his journeys in Africa, Park saw
   - (a) beavers and mink
   - (b) kangaroos and koala bears
   - (c) alligators and hippopotami.

3. After Park reached Africa he journeyed up the
   - (a) Nile River
   - (b) Great Fish River
   - (c) Gambia River.

4. Park gave a native chief gifts of
   - (a) a compass and shoes
   - (b) an umbrella and a coat
   - (c) a horse and his servant.

5. On his first journey Park had to turn back before he reached the Niger River because he fell ill with
   - (a) measles
   - (b) scurvy
   - (c) malaria.

6. On the second journey Park visited the city of
   - (a) Cairo
   - (b) Timbuctoo
   - (c) Mecca.

7. Most of the people in the city, referred to in 6, are
   - (a) Chinese
   - (b) Egyptians
   - (c) Arabs.

8. On Park's second journey, he
   - (a) did not reach the Niger River
   - (b) reached the Niger River
   - (c) sailed down the Niger River to its mouth.

THINGS TO DO TOGETHER

1. Make a list of animals found near the banks of the Niger River. Ask for volunteers to give short talks on these animals.
2. Topic for Class Discussion: Why are there not many white people living in Central Africa?
3. On a map of Africa mark in the following places: Gambia River, Niger River, Timbuctoo, Lagos, Gulf of Guinea. Show the route Park took on his second journey.

THINGS TO DO SEPARATELY

1. The natives on the banks of the Niger used shells for money. Collect specimens of money from (*a*) China (*b*) England (*c*) France (*d*) Holland (*e*) Irish Free State (*f*) United States of America.
2. Collect pictures for the class bulletin board of: African natives, Arabs, native huts and animals.

DAVID LIVINGSTONE

In 1840, three years after Queen Victoria ascended the throne, David Livingstone, a young Scottish doctor and missionary, set out for South Africa where he was destined to spend the rest of his life teaching and healing the natives and exploring the Dark Continent.

At that time little was known about the interior of Africa. Many explorers had sailed along its coast but few had gone far inland. Africa was known as a continent full of dangers from fierce tribes, from hunger, from heat, from fevers and disease. Into this land Livingstone was determined to go.

Few boys have had to endure the hardships that faced David Livingstone as a youth. He was one of a family of thirteen and his father, who was a poor tea merchant, was forced to send his son, at the age of ten, to work in a cotton mill. Here the young lad laboured from six in the morning till eight at night. After the day's work was done, David Livingstone spent each evening in study. For thirteen years he worked by day and studied at night. He then went to college and became a medical missionary.

In 1841 he arrived in Capetown, South Africa, and journeyed up through British and Dutch Colonies to a negro settlement where he spent six months learning the language of the people with whom he planned to live.

Livingstone's bravery on one occasion did much to win the love and respect of the negroes. He was told of a lion which for some weeks had been terrifying the villagers, killing their cattle and attacking women and children. Livingstone decided that he would rid the country of this killer. One day he spied the lion in the tall grass and, raising his gun to his shoulder, quickly fired both barrels at it. The lion, however, was only wounded and as Livingstone was reloading his gun the beast leapt at him. Its sharp teeth sank into his shoulder and it tossed him about "as a terrier does a rat". A negro servant seized Livingstone's gun and fired. The angry lion left Livingstone and grasped the servant in its fierce jaws. Another African who attempted to spear the great beast was in turn pounced upon and badly mauled. Then a great shiver passed through the monster's body and it fell to the ground dead. The bullets had done their work. Livingstone had been severely wounded for the lion's teeth had splintered the bones of his shoulder. In time he recovered but he carried the scars of this attack for the rest of his life.

Livingstone heard of a fertile country to the north where a fine negro tribe known as the Makalolos lived and he made plans to go there. The journey took him over a dry hot desert, known as the Kalahari Desert, where the only inhabitants were little dwarf-like bushmen. The heat was terrible. Water was very scarce. One day the party looked

far ahead and saw before them a glistening expanse which they thought was a lake. When they drew near to it they were bitterly disappointed for it was only white salt glistening in the bright sunlight. Later they reached a lake of fresh water, Lake Ngami, "a fine sheet of water," but here swarms of mosquitoes tormented them and they journeyed on. After many weeks they reached the Makalolo country and made friends with that tribe of black men who became Livingstone's trusted friends for the rest of his life. Their chief, Sekelutu, told Livingstone of a mighty river to the north and Livingstone decided to travel to it. It was the Zambezi. Livingstone determined to

EXPLORATIONS OF LIVINGSTONE
AND STANLEY

discover where it rose and into what body of water it flowed. He also wanted to find an easier way of reaching this Makalolo country than by crossing the great Kalahari Desert. Perhaps he would discover a new route by which white men could reach this rich country.

With twenty-seven sturdy Makalolos for guides he started up the river by canoe. His supplies were scanty— a few biscuits, a little tea, sugar, twenty pounds of coffee, three books, clothing and instruments. Boiled zebra, dried elephant and antelope meat were also provided from time to time by the hunters in the party. They passed through many native towns and Livingstone won the friendship of the negroes in many ways. At times he won their good-will by showing them slides from the magic lantern that he carried. Some of the native chiefs demanded payment or toll of goods for safe conduct through their country which caused Livingstone's food supplies to dwindle.

On the river banks giant hippopotami sported and long-faced crocodiles swarmed in the water. Overhead huge creepers twined from the boughs of the trees, bright strange flowers sent their heavy perfumes through the air. Livingstone travelled through dense tropical forests and hot steaming swamps infested by poisonous insects which bit and stung him. At one town, the natives gave Livingstone oxen which proved of little use, for the heavy animals sank down in the thick mud by the river bank and floundered about helplessly. Each night the faithful Makalolos who travelled with him plucked soft grass for their master's bed and after setting up his tiny tent, they slept at the door keeping watch over their friend.

Livingstone was greatly disturbed when he saw, day after day, slave-dealers driving gangs of helpless negroes to the coast to be sold as slaves. These unhappy creatures were chained together so that they could not escape. Those who lagged behind were flogged unmercifully and the sick were left to die. Along the route of the slave-traders lay the bones of the unlucky victims. Livingstone longed to help these people. He promised the natives that he would do all in his power to rid Africa of slavery.

When Livingstone reached the source of the Zambezi River he was not ready to turn back. He wished to continue westward till he reached the White Man's Sea—the Atlantic Ocean. The climate on the route had been hot and wet and Livingstone grew thin and ill. He was very weak. During the long journey he had suffered from no less than twenty-seven attacks of fever. However, as the party made its way to higher ground Livingstone's health improved. Soon a white man's trading post was sighted and here supplies of food, clothing and medicine were obtained. He and his companions rested for ten days. They learned from the traders that the little Portuguese town of Loanda on the Atlantic coast was not far away. When Livingstone reached the town he was greeted by an Englishman, a Mr. Gabriel, who offered the good doctor his bed. "Never shall I forget," wrote Livingstone, "the luxury I enjoyed in feeling myself again in a good English bed after six months sleeping on the ground."

Livingstone was offered passage home on a British warship which was in the harbour but he refused for he had promised to take the Makalolos back to their home. He feared that these black men might fall into the hands of the slave-dealers if he left them to return home alone. So he turned from the White Man's Sea on the long journey eastward. The journey there had taken six months but the homeward one took twice that time for the men were now weary and tired.

When Linyanti, the home of the Makalolos, was reached there were great celebrations. The whole town swarmed out to welcome the travellers. The men "decked themselves, in their best in suits of white and red caps which gave them a rather dashing appearance." The travellers spent many evenings telling of the places they had visited and the strange sights they had seen.

After a short rest Livingstone was on his way again. He wished now to follow the great Zambezi River eastward to its mouth. The route from the Makalolo country westward to the coast had been full of untold dangers, perhaps this route eastward would be an easier one. This time he had

THE GREATEST FALLS IN THE WORLD

no difficulty in getting guides. The Makalolos loved the Great White Doctor and wished to travel with him.

After journeying downstream for two weeks, Livingstone saw in the distance five white columns of smoke rising high into the air and he heard a roaring which grew louder and louder. He was told by his guides that they were approaching a great waterfall. Soon he gazed at the spot where a mighty river hurled itself amidst clouds of spray into a vast chasm far below. He was paddled out in a canoe to an island which hung over the crest of the falls and looked down on the greatest falls in the world, four times mightier than Niagara. From it rose great clouds of mist and vapour which the natives called "the smoke that sounds." In his diary Livingstone wrote, "It is as though the Thames at London were to plunge into a chasm and be carried along some thirty miles . . . seething and roaring between steep banks." Livingstone was the first white man to behold this wondrous sight. He named the roaring waters Victoria Falls in honour of the Queen of England.

Weakness and fever again attacked him as he journeyed on down the Zambezi. Many of the oxen which were used to carry the heavy loads were bitten by the tsetse[1] fly. The bite of these flies was death to ox or horse or dog. Food became scarce and the party was forced to live on zebras that the guides were occasionally able to shoot. One morning the weary travellers met a band of white men. They had been sent from a Portuguese settlement on the East African coast to find the Great White Doctor. They brought with them fresh supplies of food, clothing and medicine. Livingstone relates that he then sat down to "the most refreshing breakfast I ever partook of." Soon afterwards he reached the coast.

Livingstone had found an easier route by which white men could reach the Makalolo country. News of his coming had spread like wildfire through the country and crowds were waiting to meet him. An English warship took him to the British island of Mauritius where he rested before making the long journey back to England.

When he arrived home he was given a warm welcome and great honours were heaped on him. He had left his homeland sixteen years before, an unknown medical missionary; now he returned the most famous explorer of his day. Queen Victoria summoned him to Windsor Castle and

[1] Pronounced *set-see*.

from him she heard the story of his travels. Remembering his promise to do something to help the sad lot of the slaves, Livingstone spent much time speaking and writing of the "open sore of slavery." Largely because of his efforts, some years later British Africa was freed of slavery.

Two years later Livingstone again left England and sailed to a town at the mouth of the Zambezi River in Eastern Africa. With him he took a steamer which the natives nicknamed *Ma-Robert* after Mrs. Livingstone, the mother of Robert, Livingstone's eldest son. The ship had been taken to Africa in sections and was put together when the river was reached. Although the *Ma-Robert* proved useful in travelling up the Zambezi and Shire Rivers for two hundred miles it also gave much trouble for it was forever grounding on sand banks, and much time was wasted refloating it. Finally the ship was abandoned and the party started out on foot over the narrow native tracks which run in networks through the dense forests in that part of Africa. The journey led them to Lake Shirwa. Livingstone was the first white man to gaze on its water. He wrote in his diary, "It is a lake of bitter water containing leeches, fish, crocodiles and hippopotami."

Livingstone pressed on to the north to another lake of which he had heard, one that had been discovered by the Portuguese but of which little was known. Presently he reached the shores of Lake Nyassa and gazed on the majestic range of mountains to the east which are now known as the Livingstone Range. "How far is it to the end of the lake?" he inquired of a native. In reply the native said "Whoever heard of such a thing? Why if one started when a mere boy to walk to the other end of the lake, he would be an old, grey-headed man before he got there." Livingstone sent home to England for a little steamer which he planned to use on this lake. Mrs. Livingstone came to stay with her husband at the time the boat arrived. The unhealthy climate proved too much for her and six days after her arrival she took the fever and died. She was buried by her broken-hearted husband beneath a large boabab tree. Livingstone was crushed by this blow. Although he used the new steamer for a short time, he lost interest in his work and soon returned to England.

When he had rested some months, Africa called to him once more. Livingstone had crossed Africa from west to east; he now was resolved to travel from the south to the north and if possible to find the source of the Nile River and continue down its waters to the Mediterranean Sea. This time he set out from the East African coast with a party, Indians from Bombay, freed negroes, and a few of his faithful Makalolos. Camels, Indian buffaloes, mules and donkeys carried the supplies. Livingstone's little pet poodle, Chitane, accompanied the party.

The tsetse fly attacked the beasts and some died from the bites. The natives were cruel to those animals that survived and mistreated them. Finally only one young buffalo remained alive. Food was scarce and the hungry black men lagged behind, killed this last buffalo, and ate it. Afraid of what Livingstone might say they told him that the beast had died of sickness and that tigers had devoured it. Livingstone was sure they were not telling him the truth. To trick them he asked this question, "Did you see the stripes on the tiger?" They all replied, "Yes, we did." They were lying, because there were no striped tigers in Africa.

The men grew more discontented and disobedient and many refused to go any further. Some threw their loads down on the ground and returned to the coast spreading the false news that Livingstone had been killed by a band of Zulus. Livingstone and his Makalolos were left far from food and supplies in the heart of the jungle. They had only a little corn and some goat's milk. Two more disasters that upset him greatly came upon Livingstone at this time. First his faithful little dog, Chitane, while swimming through a marsh was drowned and soon after this his valuable medicine chest was stolen. With only five men left the little party struggled on. Each day Livingstone grew weaker. At last his men had to carry him in a swinging cot; but still he would not give up and return. Westwards he travelled towards the great African lakes, Nyassa and Tanganyika.

Many months passed by and no news of Livingstone reached the outside world. In the meantime people in England and the United States feared that Livingstone was dead. Nothing had been heard from him for four years. A search party was sent out by an American newspaper and Henry Stanley was chosen to lead the expedition. He was told "to bring information about Livingstone, if living, and if dead to bring home his bones." After many months of searching Stanley heard stories from the natives of a good white man who was near Lake Tanganyika. Stanley headed north determined to find if this man was Livingstone.

Meantime Livingstone lay weak and ill in a native hut. He had all but given up hope when a native came running to him and said that a great caravan was approaching headed by a man carrying the Stars & Stripes. He also related that the newcomers had bales of goods, a tin bath, and huge cooking kettles. Livingstone replied, "This must be a wealthy traveller indeed and not one at his wit's end, like me."

When Stanley entered the village he was directed to the Great White Doctor. He wrote of this famous meeting in his diary, "As I advanced slowly towards him I noticed that he was pale, looked worried, wore a bluish cap with a faded gold band round it, had on a red-sleeved waistcoat and a pair of grey tweed trousers. As I walked up to him I . . . said:

'Dr. Livingstone, I presume.'

'Yes,' he said, with a kind smile, lifting his cap. . . . We both grasped hands. I then said aloud, 'I thank God, doctor, that I have been permitted to see you.' He answered, 'I feel thankful that I am here to welcome you.' "

"DR. LIVINGSTONE, I PRESUME"

Stanley's coming cheered Livingstone greatly. Stanley begged the doctor to return home with him but Livingstone refused. He felt that his place was here among the natives who needed him. He also wished to complete his explorations and find the source of the Nile River. Stanley bade his friend good-bye and the two parted.

Next year Livingstone set out on his last journey. His health was failing fast. For nine months he and his Makalolos travelled on through endless swamps. The rainy season came on and at last Livingstone was unable to travel further. Early one morning Susi, his servant, found his master's body by the side of his bed. His head was buried in the pillow. Livingstone was dead. The sorrowing Susi buried Livingstone's heart under the shadow of a great tree and carved his name on the bark. His body was carefully embalmed, wrapped in a roll of bark, and carried for hundreds of miles to the sea-coast. A warship took the precious burden to England where Livingstone was laid to rest in Westminster Abbey.

TEST

Which word or words in Column II is closely associated with a group of words in Column I?

COLUMN I	COLUMN II
1. Town where Livingstone landed in Africa on his first journey.	(a) Tsetse fly
2. Desert in South Africa.	(b) Zambezi
3. Tribe of African natives whom Livingstone trusted.	(c) Stanley
4. Insects whose bite caused the death of many of Livingstone's oxen.	(d) Livingstone
5. An animal which nearly caused Livingstone's death.	(e) Capetown
6. River on which Victoria Falls are found.	(f) Victoria
7. Range of mountains near Lake Nyassa.	(g) Makalolo
8. Man sent to search for Livingstone.	(h) Westminster Abbey
9. Place where Livingstone was buried.	(i) Lion
10. Queen of England at that time.	(j) Kalahari

THINGS TO DO TOGETHER

1. In plasticine make a model of an African village showing the natives' huts and the date-palm trees towering above their homes. Imagine that Livingstone is paying a visit to the village and put a tiny Union Jack over his hut.
2. In plasticine model animals found in Central and South Africa (lion, giraffe, crocodile, zebra and elephant).
3. On a large blackboard map of Africa trace in the paths of the great rivers: Nile, Niger, Congo and Zambezi. Locate the following places which Livingstone visited: Lake Ngami, Lake Nyassa, Victoria Falls, Livingstone Range, Lake Tanganyika Lake Victoria Nyanza and Kalahari Desert.

4. On a strip of brown wrapping paper make a mural showing Livingstone meeting Stanley. Make your sketch in charcoal and colour it, using pastel crayons.

5. Imagine that you are a Makalolo native. Give three reasons why you love to serve David Livingstone, the Great White Doctor.

THINGS TO DO SEPARATELY

1. Diamonds are exported from South Africa. How are diamonds mined? Why are they so valuable? What are the names of two of the most famous diamonds?

2. Find out when slavery was abolished in British South Africa.

3. Find out what a tsetse fly looks like. Why was it feared by the explorers in Africa?

BOOKS TO READ

For the Teacher

The Book of the Long Trail, H. Newbolt. *Longmans, Green & Co.*

Exploration and Discovery, A. B. Archer. *Cambridge University Press.*

A History of Geographical Discovery and Exploration, J. N. Baker. *George G. Harrap & Co. Ltd.*

For the Pupil

A Book of Discovery, M. B. Synge. *Thomas Nelson & Co.*

Boys' Book of Exploration, J. Harris Gable. *E. P. Dutton & Co.*

Heroes of Exploration, R. Finch. *University of London Press.*

Map Makers, J. Cottler and H. Jaffe. *Ryerson Press.*

STANLEY ON THE CONGO

The four months that Stanley spent with Livingstone in Africa altered his whole life. From then on he resolved to be an explorer and to learn more of Africa's secrets. When David Livingstone died, Stanley took up the work which Livingstone had left unfinished. Livingstone had discovered a river in Central Africa, the Lualaba, but he did not know whether it flowed into the Nile or the Congo. This was one of the problems which Stanley hoped to solve. He also planned to journey to Lake Victoria Nyanza to find out if it was one large lake or a chain of small lakes. Thirdly, he undertook to explore the region between Lake Tanganyika and Lake Victoria Nyanza to find out if there was any waterway connecting the two.

In the year 1874, Stanley with a party of three white men, Frank and Edward Pocock, sons of an English fisherman, and a young clerk named Barker, landed in East Africa at Zanzibar. With them they had brought a great many coils of brass wire, pounds of beads, and hundreds of yards of cotton cloth which Stanley hoped to use instead of money in trading with the natives. Stanley also brought a portable boat, the *Lady Alice*, which could be easily carried in eight sections. When it was put together, it measured forty feet in length. In Zanzibar, three hundred and fifty natives were hired to act as load carriers on the journey.

The overland route from the coast to Lake Victoria Nyanza proved to be a terrible one. For one hundred and three days the party trudged through bushland in the blistering heat of the tropics. Little fresh food could be found and before many weeks had passed many of the native carriers were completely exhausted. During the

journey some of them died. One of the white men, Edward
Pocock, also died.

When the Victoria Nyanza was reached, Stanley set up
a camp where his supplies were stored. After spending only
a short time there he set out to explore the lake, aboard the
Lady Alice. The two white men, Frank Pocock and Barker,
were left in charge of the camp. Natives from the neighbouring villages distrusted the white men and tried to
discourage Stanley from sailing on their lake. They told
him that it would take years to sail around the lake; and
that fierce men with long tails lived along the shores and
that these strange creatures enjoyed eating human flesh.
Stanley paid little heed to their strange tales, however, for
he was not a man to be frightened by such things.

The *Lady Alice* passed many native villages surrounded
by groves of banana and date palm trees. At the northern
end of the lake, Stanley watched the waters of the Victoria
Nyanza rush headlong over the Ripon Falls down the Nile
towards the great sea. Many years before, the explorer,
Speke, had discovered these falls and gazed on this very
sight. To the west of the lake lay the land of Uganda. Here
Stanley landed and visited M'tesa, the powerful ruler of
that land. This friendly monarch gave Stanley a warm
welcome and entertained both the leader and his party at
court for twelve days. King M'tesa inquired about the
ways of white men and he showed great interest in hearing
about the Christian religion.

Not all of the native tribes along the shores of the Victoria Nyanza proved to be as friendly as the people of
Uganda. Trouble was in store for Stanley. A few days later,
while the *Lady Alice* was sailing past a large island, the ship
was attacked by some three hundred natives. During the
fight, the ship ran ashore on the sand and the fierce warriors
dragged it high up on the beach. Seizing the oars, they

went a short distance away to decide how they would put their thirteen captives to death. Stanley had to act quickly to save his men's lives. He commanded his handful of followers to pull the bottom boards up from the floor of the ship and use them as paddles. While he fired with his elephant gun, his men paddled the ship out into deep water. By facing danger calmly and acting wisely, Stanley had saved himself and his men from torture and death.

For fifty-seven days the *Lady Alice* sailed around the great lake a distance of over one thousand miles. During this trip Stanley found out that Victoria Nyanza was a single sheet of water and not many small lakes, as the explorer Speke had reported.

On Stanley's return to camp, bad news awaited him. Young Barker had taken sick and died. Now only two white men remained alive, Frank Pocock and Henry Stanley.

With a sad heart, Stanley broke up camp and set out to solve the second of his problems; to find if the two lakes, Victoria Nyanza and Tanganyika, were in any way connected by water. The journey from one lake to the other lay through a region of dense forests alive with wild animals. Great round-faced baboons grinned down on the party from the overhanging branches and long-tailed monkeys chattered and turned somersaults on the boughs overhead. When Lake Tanganyika was reached Stanley explored much of the coast-line. He felt he had at last found the solution to the second question and that there was no connection between the two lakes.

Now the hardest task of all lay before the explorer, to reach the Lualaba River and to find out if it was part of the Congo or the Nile.

Far to the west, the exploring party journeyed through deep forests; and at last arrived safely on the banks of the grey Lualaba at the native town of Nyangwe. This was the farthest point which David Livingstone had reached some years before. When Stanley inquired about the river, he was told by a tall black-bearded Arab trader, Tippu-Tib, that the journey downstream would be a very dangerous one. Tippu-Tib said it could only be made under the leadership of an experienced guide. He continued, "There are large boa-constrictors in the forests, suspended by their tails waiting to gobble up travellers. You cannot travel without being covered with ants and they sting like wasps. There are leopards in countless numbers. Gorillas haunt the woods. The people are man-eaters. A party of three hundred guns started for the forest and only sixty returned." This cunning Arab, dressed splendidly in clothes of spotless white, wearing a red fez and carrying a beautifully designed silver dagger, offered his services and promised that he would escort the party for sixty days' march for the enormous sum of £1,000. He also promised to provide four hundred men to act as porters. Stanley was fooled by his fine appearance and accepted his offer.

Accompanied by Tippu-Tib, the party set off. For several days their route lay through a thick forest where the intertwining branches overhead hid the sun completely from view. Even at noon the party travelled in a dim twilight. It was almost impossible to get through the thick undergrowth and a party of natives was sent ahead to cut a path through the jungle. At this rate only a few miles could be covered each day. Everyone was greatly relieved when the river was sighted once more. Stanley divided his men into two sections; one group travelled in canoes or aboard the *Lady Alice* while the others were left to make their way as best they could along the treacherous river bank. Each day the heat grew more and more unbearable; perspiration poured from the bodies of the exhausted men.

It was not strange that many fell ill. A serious epidemic broke out; many were stricken with small-pox. Stanley could not leave the sick men behind so he bargained with a native chief in a neighbouring village for a huge dug-out canoe. This was used as a hospital ship and in it sixty of the serious cases were cared for until they recovered.

Tippu-Tib had only guided the party half of the promised distance when he broke his agreement and refused to go any further. Stanley was left in the heart of Africa and, worse still, in cannibal country, with one hundred and forty-nine men and only forty guns. Furthermore, food was growing scarce and the natives in the villages along the river refused to trade. They laughed and scoffed at Stanley when he offered coils of wire and necklaces of beads in exchange for food. Stanley knew that they were man-eaters, waiting for a chance to kill all of his party. By day and by night he and his men had to be ever on the alert ready to fight back any surprise attacks. These terrible words were heard everywhere along the river banks, "Meat! Meat! Aha! Now we shall have plenty of meat." One of Stanley's men saw one hundred and eighty-six skulls of human beings lined up in a double row along the main street of one village.

One morning a roaring sound was heard far off in the distance and the party knew that it was approaching rapids and waterfalls. When they reached the rushing waters it was only with the most skilful handling that the canoes were guided through the treacherous waters amidst great jagged rocks. Through seven series of rapids the most experienced boatmen guided their frail craft. At last they could go no further for they had reached the crest of a steep waterfall. On either bank high rocky hills towered up. Only one course was open to Stanley and that was to go around the falls by land no matter how difficult it was.

Furthermore, he and his men had to carry their supplies, canoes, and the *Lady Alice* over the perilous portion of the route. Stanley decided to cut a roadway through the solid rock in order to make the journey easier for his men. This tremendous task took many days of hard labour but he planned and carried it out so well that he won the respect of every black man in his expedition. Proudly they named their leader Bula Matari, "the rock-breaker", a name which clung to him for the rest of his life. Frank Pocock suggested that the falls be named Stanley Falls in honour of their leader.

Further downstream at the village of Rubunga the weary travellers were given an unexpected and friendly welcome. They were fed on bananas and fish. It was while Stanley was resting here that he learned for the first time the important news that the river on which he was journeying was none other than the Congo.

Stanley's troubles were not over. He had reached another stretch of the river where the natives were not only unfriendly but were also well equipped with ammunition and muskets which they had obtained from traders who had come up the Congo from the Atlantic Coast. In this part of the river alone Stanley and his party fought off thirty-one fierce attacks. News of his coming reached a village long before he did, for the natives had their own method of conveying news. By beating on their huge wooden drums, the natives telegraphed warning signals from one place to another with great speed.

Everyone was thankful when the river narrowed down into a gorge for they knew that for a time they were safe from attack, as few tribesmen lived on the steep wooded hills on either bank. For four months the weary men paddled through this section of the Congo, a distance of one hundred and fifty miles. The river then widened into a broad basin of water which they named Stanley Pool and then the waters rushed headlong over another stretch of rapids to a great waterfall which was named Livingstone Falls in memory of Stanley's great friend. In this portion of the river the canoes needed to be handled in a very skilful manner. At times they were taken from the river and portages were made; at other times the more daring of the expert boatmen guided them through the menacing waters. Every day, even though the greatest of care was taken, accidents occurred. At one time three canoes and nine men were swept into the rushing waterfalls and never seen again. The saddest loss of all, however, was when Frank Pocock decided to shoot the rapids in a frail canoe. Because he was quite lame from an accident and unable to walk, he had insisted on taking the chance and headed into a very dangerous section of rapids. The canoe was caught and tossed over into the swirling whirlpool and never seen again. Pocock was Stanley's last white companion and his loss was felt very keenly not only by Stanley but also by the rest of the men. For a time a gloom seemed to descend over all of them. Many of the men refused to go further down a river which had brought only sickness, trouble, and death. Some did desert Stanley but in a few days they returned and begged his forgiveness.

Now they heard rumours that they were near the Atlantic coast. One of the villagers told Stanley of a white man, an Englishman, who some years before had reached this place from the sea. This news cheered everyone. When Stanley learned that more rapids lay ahead on the Congo he decided to leave the river and make his way overland to the ocean. His ship, the *Lady Alice,* was of no further use to him and he decided to leave it behind. "Farewell, brave boat," he cried. "Seven thousand miles up and down broad Africa thou hast accompanied me. For over five thousand miles thou hast been my home."

Staggering through the forests, the feeble, half-starved caravan of one hundred and fifty men, women, and children arrived at the little town of Boma near the Atlantic coast. The white people in the town gave a rousing welcome to Henry Stanley who for nine hundred and ninety-nine days had faced untold dangers and had journeyed across Africa from east to west. Before returning to England, he took his faithful native helpers back home to Zanzibar by the water-route round the Cape of Good Hope.

Stanley had found a new route up the Congo River into the heart of Africa. Largely because of his efforts this section was opened up to traders who came here and obtained ivory, rubber, and oils from the natives.

The work which David Livingstone had so ably begun had been completed by his friend, Henry Stanley. The two explorers, between them, had thrown open the heart of darkest Africa to the world. For Stanley's great work in Africa, he was knighted by Queen Victoria. When he died on his tombstone below his name there were carved three words. They were:

Bula Matari
Africa

TEST

Three of each set of four words are related to one another. Which ones are not?
1. Niger, St. Lawrence, Nile, Congo.
2. Baker, Pocock, Mungo Park, Stanley.
3. Victoria Nyanza, Tanganyika, Nyassa, Erie.
4. Swamps, blazing sun, jungle, frost.
5. Asbestos, ivory, rubber, palm oil.
6. Calcutta, Zanzibar, Boma, Capetown.

7. Livingstone Falls, Stanley Falls, Niagara Falls, Victoria Falls.
8. Lion, baboon, kangaroo, hippopotamus.
9. Chestnut, coco-nut, date, banana.
10. Rapids, waterfalls, whirlpool, pond.

THINGS TO DO TOGETHER

1. Plan a series of pictures on Stanley. Some of the pictures might be: Meeting Tippu-Tib, Shooting the Rapids, Fighting Back a Native Attack.

THINGS TO DO SEPARATELY

1. Get pictures of the animals that Stanley saw in Africa. Try to find out about their size, colour, and the food they eat.
2. Read a longer story about Henry Stanley. Find out about Stanley's early life. Tell the rest of the class how Stanley got his name. (He was baptized John Rowlands).

BOOKS TO READ

FOR THE TEACHER

The Book of the Long Trail, Henry Newbolt. *Longmans Green & Co.*

Exploration and Discovery, A. B. Archer. *Cambridge University Press.*

Through the Dark Continent, Henry Stanley. *Harper & Bros.*

FOR THE PUPIL

The Boys' Book of Exploration, J. Harris Gable. *E. P. Dutton & Co.*

A Book of Discovery, M. B. Synge. *Thomas Nelson & Sons, Ltd.*

The Story of H. M. Stanley, Vautier Golding. *T. C. & E. C. Jack Ltd.*

BURTON AND SPEKE

The source of the Blue Nile had been discovered by Bruce but many people believed that this river was only a branch of the main stream. The natives of Africa and the Arabs declared that the Nile probably rose from a great lake in Central Africa near the Mountains of the Moon. Richard Burton and Captain John Speke were two of the first white men to enter this region to find out if this legendary lake really existed, and if the Nile flowed out from it.

Burton, a tall, dark, lean soldier had spent many years in Arabia where he had lived a very adventurous life. Disguised as a pilgrim, he had entered Mecca, the sacred city of the Arabs, a thing no Christian was allowed to do. While in the East he had travelled in many disguises and had learned many languages. With him on this new adventure, he took Captain Speke who had been a British army officer in India for many years. Both men were well suited to undertake the dangerous journey of exploration in Central Africa.

Leaving Zanzibar, an important slave-market on the East African coast, they journeyed by caravan over the low fever-ridden flats near the ocean and, after three months hard travelling they arrived at the town of Kaze. Here Burton learned from a trader that instead of one great lake in Central Africa there were at least three. Burton and Speke determined to explore these lakes. Native guides and porters were hired. After a long and difficult journey through tropical jungles, the party arrived at the shores of a great lake named Tanganyika. Here five hundred miles inland and far from any medical care Burton fell ill with fever and had to be left in the care of some natives, while Speke, in a dugout canoe made of a heavy log, set out with twenty natives to explore the lake. He examined the northern shores and found that the Nile did not flow from this lake.

Burton was still ill when Speke returned from the trip around Lake Tanganyika. Speke was again forced to leave him. This time Speke set out to find a second and much larger lake of which he had heard, far to the north-east. With him he took thirty natives and a six weeks' supply of food. He travelled on a donkey's back and for protection he carried a great elephant gun. The native guides proved to be bad-tempered, slow and very untrustworthy and on the journey there they ate up nearly all of the precious food. All of his difficulties were quickly forgotten however when, early one morning, Speke gazed down from a high hill-top on a vast inland sea which the natives called Nyanza, meaning a great body of water. It was so broad that Speke could not see across it to the opposite shore, and it was so long that not even the natives knew its length. Speke believed that he had, at last, reached the true source of the Nile. "This magnificent sheet of water," said he, "I have ventured to name Victoria after our gracious queen." Ever since then this lake has been called Victoria Nyanza.

Food supplies were so low that Speke did not dare stay to explore the shores of Victoria Nyanza any further. He returned to Burton and told him of his great discoveries. Trouble arose between the two men for the sick man was jealous of Speke's successes. The two parted and Speke returned to Britain several months ahead of Burton.

Speke and Grant

When Speke on his return to England placed before the Royal Geographical Society his maps showing his discoveries of Lakes Tanganyika and Victoria Nyanza, the President said, "Speke, we must send you there again." With the purpose of discovering if Lake Victoria Nyanza was the source of the Nile, in 1860 Speke, with an old friend, Captain Grant, set out from England and reached Zanzibar. On the trip inland from the coast, their caravan was made up of a company of two hundred and twenty persons, Arabs, freed negro slaves and South African police. Mules and donkeys carried the heavy loads, and goats provided milk for the men. Supplies of beads, coils of brass wire and pieces of cloth were to be used as money in exchange for food, or for safe passage through a district.

Trouble followed them from the start. Many of the negroes deserted and returned to the coast. Grant and some of the South African police took fever. By the time Kaze was reached, only half of the party remained with Speke. All of the donkeys, mules and goats were dead.

In spite of disappointments and delays, Speke set out from Kaze and in a few weeks reached the south-western shores of Victoria Nyanza. He planned to travel around it to its far northern shores to find out if its waters emptied into the Nile.

On this journey a violent attack of fever seized Speke and he developed a hacking cough. He grew so thin that his legs were like match-sticks. Sick as he was, he and his men plodded on till they came to the land of a friendly king who invited them to his palace. This fine-looking black man sat cross-legged on the ground smoking a huge pipe of clay. Food was given to the strangers and no money was asked for it. The king shook hands in English style and insisted on Speke telling him all about the world, the great ships at sea and of Queen Victoria of England and her royal palaces. A great feast was held in Speke's honour.

Uganda, on the western shores of the lake, was the next country through which the explorers passed. It was a beautiful and well-cared-for land. The climate was healthy and the temperature was perfect. The natives' huts were clean and neat. M'tesa was the King of Uganda and his subjects, declaring he was the mightiest monarch in all the world, paid him great honour. Usually African natives wear very few clothes but these natives were well clothed, and even the little boys were dressed in skin cloaks which were held tightly around their legs lest anyone, by chance, might see their knees. These fine people were the most highly civilized natives Speke had yet met in Africa. After saying farewell to the tall good-looking chief, Speke wrote these words in his diary: "We rose with an English bow, placing the hand on the heart whilst saying adieu and whatever we did M'tesa in an instant mimicked with the instinct of a monkey."

The explorers moved on to the territories of a neighbouring king whose palace was a great contrast to that of M'tesa. It was merely a dirty hut and the path to it was ankle-deep in mud. The king's sisters were not allowed to marry. From morning till night they drank milk with the result that they grew so fat that it took eight men to lift one of them. The king, a poor-looking creature, was unfriendly for he had heard rumours that these white men were fierce cannibals who would attack and eat him. Speke gave the king a pair of glasses, a box of matches and some wire and the king became a little more friendly. However he made Speke remain in his land for many months and refused to give him permission to leave.

Speke was finally allowed to go. He reached the northern end of Victoria Nyanza. From here a river flowed out of the lake. "Perhaps," thought Speke, "this is the Nile!" It was. Speke had reached the spot where the waters of the Victoria Nyanza poured into the river. A few miles down the river, he came to a broad waterfall, and there watched tons of frothy bubbling water hurl itself over the rocks. Thousands of fish leaped up the falls trying to get to the

waters above, while on the banks hippopotami and crocodiles lay stretched out, sleeping and sunning themselves.
With much pleasure Speke told his men to, "bathe in the
waters of this holy river, the cradle of Moses."

TWO WHITE MEN WERE APPROACHING

Having no boats, Speke and Grant were forced to travel
along the river bank. In a few days they came to the town
of Gondokoro. "Then a strange thing happened," said
Speke. "We saw hurrying on towards us the form of an
Englishman and the next moment my old friend Baker
seized me by the hand. What joy this was I can hardly
tell." Baker and his wife had set out from Cairo and had
travelled down the Nile expressly to meet Speke. Baker
had brought armed men for protection; camels, donkeys and
horses to carry his supplies when he was forced to

journey overland and also three boats which contained quantities of food and clothing. Rumours had reached Baker's ears that two white men were approaching and he felt sure that they would be his friends Speke and Grant. In his log-book Baker wrote these words of their meeting, "I ran and soon met them. They had come from the Victoria Nyanza. Speke appeared to me the more worn of the two. He was very lean; he had walked the whole way from Zanzibar. Grant was in rags—his bare knees projecting through the remnants of his trousers."

After hearing all the news from home and receiving supplies, Speke and Grant continued up the Nile to Cairo where they joined a ship bound for England. They arrived home after an absence of three years and fifty-one days. They believed that they had found the source of the Nile but in this they were partly wrong. They had found one source. Others remained to be found.

BAKER

Another Englishman who became interested in the Nile was Samuel Baker. He had been for many years a traveller in tropical lands. When his friend Speke set out to find the source of the Nile, Baker planned to journey up the river from its mouth to its source and meet Speke on the way. Baker's wife insisted on accompanying him, a thing quite unheard of in those Victorian days. "I implored her to remain in England," he writes. "I painted the difficulties and terrors but she was resolved to share all the dangers and to follow me through each rough footstep of the wild life before me." Thus he set out from Cairo with three ships on which were donkeys, camels, horses and supplies of food and clothing.

Two weeks after he and his wife reached Gondokoro, a town far up the Nile, his two friends Grant and Speke arrived. From them he learned of a lake far to the west of Victoria Nyanza which they had heard of but had been unable to visit because of their weakness and lack of food. Baker determined to journey there and find out if this lake was another source of the Nile.

Baker set out. "I led the way, Mrs. Baker riding by my side and the British flag following close behind us as a guide for the caravan of heavily laden camels and donkeys," he wrote in his journal. Before long many of the porters deserted. Further bad luck followed them. Both Baker and his wife were seized with fever, probably malaria. When food became scarce, they both had to live on native food.

When they recovered from the fever, they decided to continue the journey. One morning very early, Baker, from the summit of a high hill, saw before him a sea of blue water and in the distance a row of misty blue mountains. This was the lake he had set out to find. "I called this lake Albert Nyanza in memory of Queen Victoria's late husband," he says. He continues, "The Victoria and the Albert lakes are the two sources of the Nile. No European foot had ever trod upon its sands, nor had the eyes of any white man ever scanned its waters."

He and his wife procured a dug-out canoe from the natives and paddled along its shores. They journeyed for days. At times they used a plaid shawl which Mrs. Baker had brought from Scotland, for a sail. After a journey of thirteen days, they reached the place where the waters of the lake flowed into the Nile. Further down the river, they came to a mighty waterfall. They were forced to leave the river and travel along its banks on the backs of oxen. Mrs. Baker took ill from sun-stroke and had to be carried on a litter by the native porters. The only food left to eat was a black porridge made from mouldy bitter flour. For weeks they existed on this miserable diet, growing weaker daily. At last when Baker felt that he could go no further, he handed his headman valuable maps and papers telling of his journey and instructed the native to take them up the Nile to the English Consul in Cairo. He hoped that others might know of his successful journey even though he never lived to report about it himself.

A friendly chief, however, heard of the white man's plight. He provided the Bakers with food and shelter and helped them to make their way back to Gondokoro. When Baker and his wife finally arrived in Cairo they were given a great welcome by the English people who had believed them lost.

The sources of the White Nile were at last known. They were Victoria Nyanza discovered by Speke, Albert Nyanza discovered by Baker, and Edward Nyanza discovered a few years later by Stanley.

TEST

Which of the following statements are true, and which are false?

1. Burton and Speke set out to discover the source of the Niger River.

2. Two lakes that they discovered were Lake Tanganyika and Lake Victoria Nyanza.

3. Nyanza is a native African word which means a great body of water.

4. When Speke and Grant reached Uganda, they found that it was a very backward country.

5. Speke and Grant found that the Nile flowed out of Lake Victoria Nyanza.

6. On his journey in Africa Baker was accompanied by his wife.

7. Baker found that another source of the Nile River was Lake Albert Nyanza.

8. Burton, Speke and Baker were explorers from the United States of America.

THINGS TO DO TOGETHER

1. Make a map of Africa. Locate the following places: Nile River, Lake Victoria Nyanza, Lake Albert Nyanza, Lake Edward Nyanza, Lake Tanganyika, Cairo.

2. Using charcoal and coloured chalk make a series of large illustrations. Here are some suggestions.

   (a) Speke in a dug-out canoe exploring Lake Tanganyika.
   (b) A native village in Uganda.
   (c) Hippopotami and alligators on the banks of the Nile.
   (d) Baker and his party travelling on the backs of camels.

3. Write an interesting statement about each of the following: Zanzibar, hippopotamus, malaria, Lake Tanganyika, King M'tesa of Uganda.

4. Class Discussion: Why were many explorers afraid to travel into Central Africa?

THINGS TO DO SEPARATELY

1. Collect pictures of animals of Central Africa. Paste them into your Social Studies Scrap Book. Print the name of the animal under each of the pictures.

2. Collect coloured pictures of natives of (1) Africa (2) China (3) Japan (4) India (5) Arabia (6) New Zealand (7) England (8) Holland. Note the differences in: (a) colour of hair (b) colour of skin (c) shape of face (d) shape of eyes.

BOOKS TO READ

FOR THE TEACHER

A History of Geographical Discovery and Exploration, J. N. Baker. *George G. Harrap & Co. Ltd.*

Stories of Exploration and Discovery, Arthur Archer. *Cambridge University Press.*

FOR THE PUPIL

The Book of Discovery, T. C. Bridges. *George G. Harrap & Co. Ltd.*

A Book of Discovery, M. B. Synge. *Thos. Nelson & Sons, Limited.*

Heroes of Discovery, R. J. Finch. *University of London Press.*

Map Makers, J. Cottler and H. Jaffe. *Ryerson Press.*

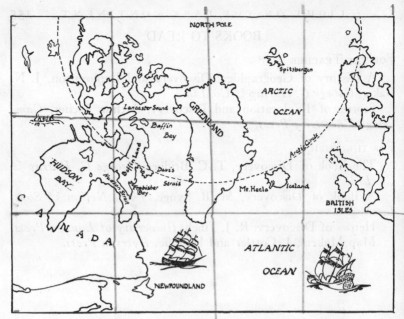

EXPLORATION IN THE ARCTIC—FROBISHER, BAFFIN,
DAVIS AND HUDSON

VI. THE SEARCH FOR THE NORTH-WEST
PASSAGE

MARTIN FROBISHER

ON a warm spring morning in the year 1576, the English
queen, Elizabeth, waved farewell from her palace on
the banks of the Thames River to Captain Martin
Frobisher, as he set out to find a new route to Cathay. His
ships were the *Gabriel*, the *Michael* and one small pinnace.
On board was a crew of thirty-five men.

Explorers from other lands had already found sea-routes
to Cathay and the East; Magellan had sailed through the
straits at the tip of South America and on across the

Pacific to the Spice Islands, and Vasco da Gama had opened up a route for Portugal by rounding the Cape of Good Hope and reaching India. Now the Englishman, Frobisher, was determined that he would find a north-west passage from the Atlantic to the Pacific in the icy regions north of America.

Battered about by many storms, the little vessels reached the fog-bound shores of Greenland and found the coast so packed with ice that they were unable to get close to the shore. The little pinnace was lost with all hands during a storm, and the commander of the *Michael,* frightened by the fierce gales, deserted and returned with his ship to England. Two weeks later Frobisher sighted the dreary shores of Labrador. Here again ice prevented him from going ashore. One morning, a huge iceberg, which suddenly loomed up through the fog, fell apart close to the ship and made such a noise that the sailors declared it sounded as if a great cliff had broken away from the land and had crashed into the sea.

When an opening in the coast appeared, Frobisher sailed into it hoping that it would lead to the passage to the Pacific. On an island near the shore, he found nineteen strange-looking people who had black hair, broad faces, flat noses, brown skins and were wearing clothes made of fur. These were Eskimos, the natives of the north. At first ice choked the passage and held Frobisher back. Later he was able to sail up what seemed to be a wide strait. He was sure that the land on his right was the continent of Asia. What he really discovered was not a strait but Frobisher Bay on the south-east coast of Baffin Island.

When a party of men from the ship landed, they bartered with the Eskimos receiving seal-skins and bear-skins in exchange for mirrors, bells and toys. Five Englishmen who ventured further inland were seized by the natives and never heard of again. Frobisher was anxious to take an Eskimo back to show to the queen and he captured one by dangling a gaily-coloured bell before the native's eyes and seizing him while he was off his guard. In his fright, the Eskimo shut his mouth so quickly that he bit off the end of his tongue.

The ice was closing in around the ship and Frobisher, fearing that he might be forced to spend the winter there if he delayed longer, turned homeward, taking with him some flowers, grasses, fur-skins and pieces of black stone which sparkled brightly in the sunlight. On the way back the Eskimo developed a cold. He died a few days after reaching England. Queen Elizabeth praised Frobisher for the success of his journey and urged him to make plans for another. She felt sure that the passage Frobisher had found was the water route to China. When goldsmiths examined the pieces of black rock that Frobisher had brought back, they stated that there was gold in it. Because of this, men, eager to get rich, begged to sail with Frobisher on his second voyage.

The next spring, three ships sailed from England and took the same course as on the first voyage. When they reached Frobisher Bay, the men immediately set to work to search for the precious black rock. Eskimos came to the ships in their tiny boats to trade. These little boats, made of seal-skins, with a keel of wood, are still used by the Eskimos to-day. They are known as *kayaks*.

Little more was learned about the passage on this trip for the men spent their time getting over two hundred tons of rock into the ships. When they sailed back to England they found, to their bitter disappointment, that the ore contained little gold. Good Queen Bess, however, praised Frobisher and gave him a chain of gold. She promised to fit out several ships for a third expedition.

Fifteen ships set sail on the third voyage. On board there were forty sailors, thirty miners and thirty soldiers. Plans had been made to start a settlement on the shores of the new land. Fearful gales blew the ships far to the south of Frobisher Bay, and they were driven up a broad body of water which led westward. Without knowing it, Frobisher had entered Hudson Strait and had discovered the first part of the passage to Cathay. During the storm several ships were lost and, when the weather cleared, the damaged ships limped back to Frobisher Bay for repairs. There again they took on a huge cargo of the black ore. No settlement was started, for the Englishmen feared the long cold Arctic winter in this desolate land and all returned to England.

Three voyages had been made and yet no passage had been found. More interest had been shown in searching for gold than in exploring. All the tons of rock which they had brought back had proved to be valueless. Discouraged at his failures, Frobisher gave up his search for the water route in the cold regions of the north. He was a good leader and a fearless explorer. His was the first attempt by an Englishman to find a north-west passage to China.

TEST

Supply the missing words in the story. The correct words are listed below the paragraph.

Martin Frobisher, an Englishman, made ———— attempts to find a water route to the East. His plan was to find a ———— passage from the Atlantic Ocean to the Pacific Ocean. On the first voyage, he sighted the coasts of ———— and Labrador but no landings were made. Later Frobisher found a wide passage which he believed would lead to the East but it was only a deep bay in what to-day is known as ———— Island. This bay has been named ———— Bay. Natives of the north, the ————, gave seal-skins and ———— to Frobisher in exchange for ————

and bells. On later voyages Frobisher was ———— in finding a passage to the East.

Greenland, Baffin, Eskimos, three, Frobisher Bay, mirrors, North-west, bear-skins, unsuccessful.

THINGS TO DO TOGETHER

1. Make a list of animals found in the northern parts of the world. Place pictures of these animals on the class bulletin board. Have different members of the class prepare talks on these animals.
2. On a wall map, locate the places mentioned in the story.

THINGS TO DO SEPARATELY

1. Frobisher believed that he had found great quantities of gold ore. Find at least three places in the world where gold is mined to-day.
2. During what months of the year does the sun never shine in the most northern parts of the world?

JOHN DAVIS

A few years after Frobisher's third voyage, two little vessels, the *Sunshine* and the *Moonshine,* sailed from England under the command of a sailor of Devon, John Davis. He too, was bent on reaching Cathay by a north-western route. With few delays the ships reached the snow-covered mountains of Greenland. Because it seemed so grim and gloomy in these silent wastes, Davis named it the "Land of Desolation." Rounding the southern tip of this land, which Davis named Cape Farewell, he sailed along its western coast. The Eskimos were shy at first, but when they heard music coming from the English ships they swarmed out in their little kayaks and crowded on board

anxious to hear more of these weird sounds. The natives'
furs were exchanged for English knives and nails. Davis
learned from the Eskimos of a vast sea to the north-west
and he headed his ships in that direction, hoping to find the
passage to Cathay. In a few days he crossed the great wide

THE ESKIMOS CAME OUT IN TINY KAYAKS

strait now named for him and reached the opposite shore
where he and his men found four huge white polar bears
and a raven, but no signs of human life. Some little
flowers like primroses were found in a sheltered place in the
rocks but no other plants of any kind. Food was getting
scarce at this time, and the men began to grumble, so Davis
decided to return to England with the encouraging news
that "a North-west Passage is a matter nothing doubtful."

The next summer found Davis again sailing along the
coasts of Greenland and Labrador. At first when the
weather was warm and the sea fairly free from ice great
swarms of mosquitoes attacked the sailors and caused
itching and lumps to rise on their skins. Tall glistening
icebergs sailed majestically by the ship and were of such a
size that Davis afterwards refused to talk very much about
them for, he said, no one would believe him if he did. Again

fields of ice drove him back and after sailing along the shores of Labrador he returned home with a cargo of cod-fish and five hundred seal-skins.

A third time Davis set out with three ships in 1587. Two of the vessels were left to fish for cod off Labrador while Davis, with a party of seamen, made his way northwards

AMIDST THE FIELDS OF ICE

up Davis Strait in an open channel. Greenland lay on his right hand and a bright blue sea, free from ice, lay to the north and west. Now and again a towering iceberg with its snowy peaks pointing to the sky floated past his ship. On and on, day after day, he sailed till he reached the far northern waters which were later named Baffin Bay. His hopes soared for he felt that he had found the channel that would lead him to the Pacific.

By next morning, however, a gale from the north had carried before it a mighty bank of ice eight feet in depth. It stretched across the strait and although Davis tried many times to push through it he found it was impossible to make any progress. With a sad heart he turned his ship home.

People in England grumbled and said, "This man has made three trips. Why hasn't he found his much-discussed passage?" Poor Davis! Although he begged for ships and money for another trip, his words fell on deaf ears and he was forced to give up his dreams of reaching Cathay. Davis however had learned many things about the northern regions. He had sailed for over seven hundred miles up the west coast of Greenland, he had explored the whole coast of Labrador and he had stated his belief that all the northern part of America was a mass of islands. In this he was later found to be correct.

TEST

Choose the correct word from those in the bracket.

1. Davis set out to find a sea-route to the East around the north of (America, Russia).
2. He named a grim, gloomy land he sighted (Land of Desolation, Land of Fire).
3. Davis named the southern tip of this land (Cape of Good Hope, Cape Farewell).
4. On the second voyage, Davis and his sailors suffered from bites from (polar bears, mosquitoes).
5. Davis Strait lies between (Greenland and Baffin Island, Labrador and Baffin Island).
6. When Davis returned from his second voyage he brought back (cod-fish and seal-skins, Eskimos and gold).
7. Davis was hindered on his voyages by the (Arctic darkness, great masses of ice).
8. Davis stated that he believed that the northern part of America was a (solid body of land, mass of islands).

THINGS TO DO TOGETHER

1. With crayons, draw pictures on a long sheet of wrapping paper to show scenes from this story. The landing of Davis in Greenland, the Eskimos coming out in their kayaks to meet Davis, and Davis' ship making its way through masses of icebergs would all make interesting pictures. Such a series of illustrations is called a frieze.

2. Davis brought back five hundred seal-skins on his second voyage. Discuss the sealing industry which is carried on off the coasts of Newfoundland and Labrador.

THINGS TO DO SEPARATELY

1. Visit a local zoo and observe the polar bear, a native of the northern parts of the world. Note the size of the bear, colour of its fur, length of its fur, its food and any interesting habits that you may notice.

2. On a map of North America study the islands, bays and straits along its northern shores.

HENRY HUDSON

Three times already Henry Hudson had ventured into far-away seas searching for a northern passage. From the first two trips he had returned disappointed, for snow, ice and storms had held him back. On his third voyage he had changed his course and had reached the shores of America sailing up the great Hudson River which was named for him, searching for the sea-route to the Pacific.

His fourth and last voyage was made on the vessel, *Discovery*. In 1610 he set sail from England bound for the north with his only son, Jack, a lad of about twelve years of age on board and a crew of discontented sailors. As they approached Iceland, he and his men saw great clouds of smoke and red-hot lava pouring down the sides of an active volcano, Mount Hecla. On shore they watched Icelanders cooking food in the hot springs that bubbled up from the rocks. After they passed Greenland, they fought a grim battle against the dangerous fields of floating ice in Davis Strait. As the long summer days passed, the *Discovery* sailed on and at last reached a wide channel which stretched far to the west. Hudson named the channel Hudson Strait. His heart beat with joy for he felt that, in a few days at the most, he would reach the peaceful waters of the Pacific and that the dreams of many years would at last be realized. For three months he searched amongst the many islands and along the shores for his ocean. It was a vain search. What he had reached was the great land-locked bay which we now call Hudson Bay.

When the cold weather set in, the waters froze around his little ship and the days of darkness came. The little group of frightened men moved to the shore where they built a rough hut of driftwood in preparation for the winter that lay ahead. In early winter ptarmigan, white partridges, and other birds were fairly plentiful and provided enough to eat, but as the long months dragged on the men began to suffer from hunger. The zero weather caused many severe cases of frost-bite and some lost fingers and toes. The men were at last forced to boil moss and eat the weak watery soup. During all this time, the only living creature they saw was an Indian who came to their winter quarters bringing with him skins of deer and beaver. Although the starving men believed that he would come back bringing help, the Indian was never seen again.

The crew of the *Discovery*, always discontented, now became mutinous. They made plans to seize control of the ship at the first opportunity and return to England as soon as the ice began to break. When spring came, Hudson tried to urge them to strike for the west again. "Come on," said he, "in a few days we will be in the Pacific." Wild with rage at their leader's stubbornness in wishing to go on, instead of returning home, they planned open mutiny. They locked up the loyal men in their cabins and seized Hudson and his son as they stepped from their stateroom one morning. A

LEFT TO THE MERCY OF THE WIND AND WAVES

row-boat was lowered and into it they put Hudson, his son, and the sick men amongst the crew. The loyal ship's carpenter and another man who had escaped from their cabins rushed up on deck to help Hudson. They, too, were seized and thrown into the little boat. With barely any provisions, some powder, some shot, a gun and an iron pot of meal, the helpless men, nine in all, were set adrift and left to the mercy of the wind and the waves. To this day, no man knows what happened to Hudson, his son and the other men.

As the crew watched the little boat drift away, they said, "There will be more food for the rest of us now that those sick and worthless fellows have gone. As for that dreamer, Hudson, he was only taking us to certain death." On the way back, several of the mutineers landed on the shore of Labrador, searching for food, and were attacked and killed by Eskimos. The journey home across the Atlantic was long and stormy. The men were so hungry that they were forced to eat candle grease. When they finally reached England, they were tried and imprisoned.

Hudson's charts and log-book were on the *Discovery* when she reached home from the journey that cost him his life. Rescue ships were sent out to search for him but without success. The silent north still holds the secret of Hudson's fate.

TEST

In sentences, write answers to the following questions:

1. Why did Hudson want to find a North-west Passage?
2. At what time of the year did Hudson start out from England on his fourth voyage? Why did he choose this time of year?
3. Hudson saw the volcano, Mount Hecla, when he visited Iceland. What is a volcano?
4. Where did Hudson and his crew spend the winter?
5. Why were his crew very discontented during the winter?
6. What did Hudson wish to do when the warmer weather came?
7. What did the crew do to Hudson when they mutinied?
8. What do you think happened to Hudson and his son?

THINGS TO DO TOGETHER

1. A word game. In the story, these words were used. For each word used in Column 1 there is a phrase that gives its meaning in Column 2. Find the group of words in 2 that belongs with each word in 1.

COLUMN 1   COLUMN 2

strait   —white partridge

explore   —men rebelling against their leader

ptarmigan —travel in little-known lands in order to discover new facts about them.

mutiny   —narrow body of water connecting two larger bodies.

log-book   —book in which daily accounts of the voyage are kept.

2. On a blank map of North America mark in Hudson's route on his last voyage. Print the names of the following places in their correct locations: Atlantic Ocean, Mount Hecla, Davis Strait, Hudson Strait, Hudson Bay, Labrador.

THINGS TO DO SEPARATELY

1. Find the famous picture showing Hudson and some of his men when they were cast adrift in Hudson Bay. Show this picture to the rest of your class.

2. Read the story of Henry Hudson's first three voyages. Plan to read or tell parts of it to your class mates.

3. In the United States of America there is a great river named for Hudson. Locate this river and find out what famous city is at the mouth of the Hudson River.

BOOKS TO READ

For the Teacher

Great Navigators and Discoverers, J. A. Brendon. *George G. Harrap & Co. Ltd.*

Stories of Exploration and Discovery, Arthur Archer. *Cambridge University Press.*

For the Pupil

Book of Polar Exploration, Edith L. Elias. *George G. Harrap & Co. Ltd.*

A Book of Seamen, F. H. Doughty. *Jonathan Cape Limited.*

Famous Voyages of Great Discoverers, Eric Wood. *George G. Harrap & Co. Ltd.*

Heroes of Discovery, R. J. Finch. *University of London Press.*

Map Makers, J. Cottler and H. Jaffe. *Ryerson Press.*

They Went Exploring, Arensa Sondergaard. *Harper & Bros.*

WILLIAM BAFFIN

Many people believed that Hudson Strait was the channel which led to the western sea. Two years after Henry Hudson's tragic voyage, another expedition from England set out to find Hudson Strait and make its way through the long-sought North-west Passage to the Pacific. The commander of the expedition was Robert Bylot, but its work is best remembered because of the pilot and recorder of the voyage, William Baffin. Baffin, who had already made four voyages into the polar seas, was an experienced seaman and a careful navigator.

Before the vessel, *Discovery,* set out, her captain was instructed to proceed from England to Greenland and from there to head into Hudson Strait. In early May, the ship reached the bleak, cheerless shores of Greenland and, sailing on to the west, it arrived in Hudson Strait and entered it, keeping close to the northern shore of the waterway. The land to the north of the Strait was ice-bound and rocky. It was later found to be part of a great island which was named Baffin Land in honour of the pilot of the expedition. The *Discovery* dropped anchor and a landing was made in this dreary, desolate land. Numbers of Eskimos shyly greeted the white men and showed them their summer homes which were rude tents made of seal-skins. Baffin reported in his log-book that the Eskimos used great husky dogs to pull the sledges. As the vessel continued on its way westward it met with great masses of ice which continually held it back and made progress difficult. At last the ship was able to go no further.

The place at which the *Discovery* finally stopped was named Cape Comfort. This cape lay beside what was thought to be a great land-locked bay. The leaders of the expedition discussed whether they should attempt to con-

tinue westward or return home. They believed that there
was no passage to the western sea by way of this route
and they decided that it would be a waste of time to continue further in this direction. When they returned to
England they reported that they had been unable to find
the North-west Passage by way of Hudson Strait but they
proudly reported that there had been no serious illness nor
loss of life during the entire voyage. This was an achieve-
ment for, in those times, a seaman's diet was made up
chiefly of salt pork. During long voyages the sailors often
fell victims of a disease known as scurvy.

One year later the *Discovery* again set sail. Plans were
made to reach Greenland and then to follow the route taken
up the western coast of Greenland by John Davis. The
captain promised to bring back a Japanese native if he was
fortunate enough to make his way through the polar seas
to Japan. After crossing the stormy North Atlantic and
reaching Greenland the sturdy vessel made its way up
Davis Strait, reaching and passing the farthest point which
Davis had reached. Although it was the month of June the
weather was so cold that the sails and ropes were frozen
stiff and the crew had the greatest of difficulty handling
them. On to the north the ship sailed, putting in to every
bay and channel in its search for the long-sought passage.
In one great bay, dozens of whales were sighted sporting in
the water. To it Baffin gave the name, Whale Sound. Great
fields of ice from the north forced the *Discovery* to change
its course and turn back but not before the ship had reached
the most northern tip of a great new expanse of water
known as Baffin Bay. No white man had ever before sailed
into these far northern waters.

On the way back, the *Discovery* sailed along the western
side of the great bay. All of the sounds along the coast
were filled with ice and the vessel was unable to proceed

into any of them. Baffin named these bays after men in England who had given money and help in preparing for the journey. Jones Sound and Lancaster Sound still bear the names of Baffin's friends. If the *Discovery* had been able to sail through Lancaster Sound, it would have reached the gateway to a series of waterways which would have led the vessel to the western sea. Unfortunately, a great wall of solid ice forced the *Discovery* to turn back.

The lack of sunshine and the diet of salt pork caused many of the crew on this voyage to fall ill with scurvy. The sailors were so sick that they were unable to do their share of the work. Baffin knew that there was a certain type of plant known as scurvy grass which grew in Greenland and which was said to cure scurvy. Orders were given to return to Greenland where quantities of this grass were gathered and fed to the sick men. In a short time many of the sailors recovered.

When Baffin presented a report of his journey in England, he again was forced to say that he had been unable to find the North-west Passage. He also stated that he believed there was no such channel to the north of Davis Strait which would lead to the great western ocean. We now know that he was mistaken.

Although Baffin had failed both times to find the passage, the voyages he had undertaken were not without result. He had discovered the vast northern sea now known as Baffin Bay and he had made friends with the Eskimos on the island now known as Baffin Land. For the next two hundred years no other English explorers continued the work so ably begun by Davis, Hudson and Baffin.

TEST

Fill in the blanks with the correct word or words.

William Baffin tried to find a ———— Passage from the Atlantic to the Pacific. On the first voyage he sailed north-west from England to Greenland and then headed west to ————— Strait. He landed on ————— Island where he made friends with the —————. These people showed him their summer homes which were made of seal-skins. Continuing in a westerly direction he reached a point of land which he named Cape —————. Here the men rested and after deciding that there was no passage in this direction, they returned to Britain.

One year later Baffin made another voyage. This time he followed the route taken by another Arctic explorer, ————— —————. He sailed north as far as Baffin Bay, sailing along the coast and naming many of the inlets after friends in England. All the inlets, he found, were blocked with —————. If Baffin had sailed up ————— Sound he might have found the long-sought passage. Many of the crew fell ill with ————— because they had eaten too much ————— —————. Baffin was forced to return home without hopeful news of a northern water-route to —————.

THINGS TO DO TOGETHER

1. Make a series of murals showing the following scenes:
    (a) Baffin's meeting with the Eskimos on Baffin Island.
    (b) Baffin's men standing on the deck of their ship and view-ing the whales in Whale Sound, Greenland.
    (c) His ship trying to make its way up ice-blocked Lancaster Sound.
2. Baffin saw whales in a bay in north-western Greenland. Make a study of the life history of a whale. Of what uses are whales to man? What British island in the South Atlantic is a centre for the whaling industry?

THINGS TO DO SEPARATELY

1. During what months of the year do icebergs menace ships travelling from Canada to Britain? What have the govern-ments of Canada and the United States done to lessen this danger?
2. Inquire and find out how the use of aeroplanes will change the life of the Eskimos on Baffin Island.

BOOKS TO READ

FOR THE TEACHER

A History of Geographical Discovery and Exploration, J. N. L. Baker. *George G. Harrap & Co. Ltd.*

FOR THE PUPIL

Boys' Book of Exploration, J. Harris Gable. *E. P. Dutton & Co.*

Book of Discovery, T. C. Bridges. *George G. Harrap & Co. Ltd.*

Book of Discovery, M. B. Synge. *Thomas Nelson & Sons.*

Book of Polar Exploration, Edith L. Elias. *George G. Harrap & Co. Ltd.*

JOHN FRANKLIN

Two hundred years later John Franklin and a party of six Englishmen set out from Hudson Bay to travel by land and water to the shores of the Arctic Ocean and explore the coast. They travelled through Northern Canada on the rivers and lakes, using frail birch-bark canoes. Often they came to rapids and waterfalls and then portages had to be made. The men had to unload the supplies and carry the canoes and the provisions along the river banks until they could relaunch the canoes. At night the men slept in buffalo-robes on the cold, hard ground.

Bitter winds from the north froze the streams and lakes and the men were forced to journey over the snow using snow-shoes and sledges. With winter came a scarcity of food and Franklin was thankful when he reached a settlement on the shores of Lake Athabaska. Here the party rested during the long, cold months.

When the ice melted in spring, the party set out, once

again, down the Great Slave River and reached Great Slave
Lake. Indians guided the men through the lake, down the
Yellow River, and on into Winter Lake. On the shores of
this lake Franklin and his men built a log hut and named it
Fort Enterprise. They spent the second winter there making

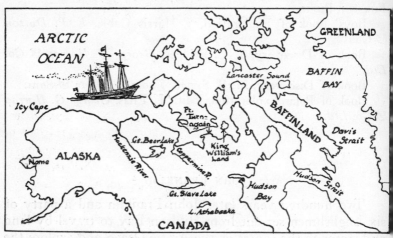

FRANKLIN'S EXPLORATIONS IN THE ARCTIC

plans for their trip to the Arctic Ocean in the spring. The
cold was so great that the wood which they used for fuel
became so hard that it broke the axes the men used for
chopping it. Tea froze in the pots before it could be drunk.
Food, however, was easily found. There were herds of
reindeer on land and fine salmon in the rivers. An Indian
chief promised Franklin that he would put a large supply
of food in the fort, so that the party would have plenty
when it returned from the Arctic. By June the ice had
broken up enough to allow them to travel by water and the
party, leaving the fort, headed north for the Arctic Ocean.

By canoe, they travelled down the rivers and through
numberless lakes till they came to the swift, dangerous

waters of the Coppermine River. Many rapids and falls delayed their progress and portages again had to be made. Swarms of mosquitoes attacked and tormented them by day and night and caused great discomfort to the men.

At last, the shores of the Arctic Ocean were reached and Franklin gazed out on its vast, frigid waters. He and his party then turned eastward to explore the coast. The only boats that they had were birch-bark canoes and these proved very dangerous craft, for the sea was quite open. Although the canoes were kept near shore where the water was fairly calm, they were in constant danger of being crushed by masses of moving ice or of being pierced by sunken rocks. Deer, bears, musk-oxen, white foxes, swans, geese, seals, and fish were plentiful and provided food for the explorers. Thus they made their way along the shore for a distance of five hundred miles, exploring rivers, capes, and bays, and naming them for friends at home. With winter approaching, Franklin decided to return to Fort Enterprise for he dared not go further. The place where he turned back was named Point Turnagain. He planned to take a shorter route by land for food was growing scarce and he thought that his men might shoot more game on the overland route. As they set out, a gale blew for many days. Winter had set in earlier than was expected. The rivers froze and the men were unable to use their canoes. Deep banks of snow slowed up their progress. In spite of these obstacles they struggled on. Game was scarce and the small supply of biscuits and dried meats that they had with them was soon used up. At last, the men were forced to cut up scraps of leather and old shoes and make them into a weak soup. Even the horns and bones of a deer were cooked and eaten by the starving men.

The only thing that kept them from giving up was the thought of the food waiting for them at Fort Enterprise.

Imagine their heart-break when they arrived at the fort and found it empty! The place was deserted and not a scrap of food was to be found. The Indian chief had not kept his promise. For eighteen terrible days, the starving men lay in the fort. Their only food was a thin soup made from the skin of a deer. The men's legs grew so swollen that they could walk no more than a few steps. Days passed and they grew weaker and weaker. One morning a herd of deer passed near the fort but so exhausted were the men that they were unable to lift their guns to shoot.

Two of the sick men died and the end seemed near for the others. Then, one morning, as if by a miracle, three Indians, hunting game, walked into the hut. They arrived not a moment too soon. The Indians at once prepared food for the men and built a cheerful fire for them. For several weeks they stayed at the fort and nursed the Englishmen back to health again. When Franklin and his men were well enough to travel back to Hudson Bay, the Indians accompanied them for a good part of the way. From Hudson Bay, Franklin and his party sailed back to England after a journey that had taken them almost three years.

Six years later Franklin returned to Canada to explore more of the Arctic coast. He travelled overland by canoe and dog team until he reached the shores of Great Bear Lake. His men built a hut there and named it Fort Franklin in honour of their commander. A few of the men stayed at the fort while Franklin and the others travelled by boat till they reached the wide, swift Mackenzie River. They found the journey down this river much easier than their trip down the Coppermine River. As it neared the ocean, the river broke into many channels or mouths. By late summer, the party reached the Arctic Ocean where, in honour of the occasion, Franklin unfurled a silken Union Jack and his men cheered and drank the health of the king.

As it was too late in the season to do any further exploring the party returned to Fort Franklin for the winter.

In late June, they started out again with four boats and enough food to last them for eighty days. At the mouth of the Mackenzie River the party divided; one group was sent east to explore the coast as far as the Coppermine River while Franklin and the other group sailed west. Next morning Franklin reached a large settlement of three hundred Eskimos who came out in their little kayaks to gaze at the strange white men. As Franklin travelled further along the coast he found many more Eskimo settlements. Past river mouths, bays, and islands he travelled till he came near Icy Cape, but he dared go no further to the west for the fogs were thick and the sea was full of ice. He returned to Fort Franklin before winter set in. If he had travelled west only a hundred miles further he would have met a ship which had come from the Pacific to greet him but this he did not know.

At Fort Franklin he was joined by the party which had successfully journeyed eastward along the Arctic coast as far as the Coppermine River and had mapped out over nine hundred miles of the shore.

On his return to England, Franklin received a knighthood from the king.

Many years later at the age of fifty-eight Franklin again offered his services to England to head an expedition to settle once and for all the question of the North-west Passage. He sailed from England with a crew of one hundred and twenty-nine men, picked from the Royal Navy, aboard two ships, the *Erebus* and *Terror*. These ships had been fitted with steam engines to give them extra power. The ships carried sufficient supplies to last for several years. So sure was Franklin of success that he wrote to a friend saying, "Write to Panama and the Sandwich

Islands every six months. Your letters will reach us there."

After an excellent voyage across the Atlantic Ocean, Sir John Franklin reached Disko Island off the west coast of Greenland. A supply ship carried letters full of hope and cheer back to Britain and then the *Erebus* and *Terror* headed west across Baffin Bay to Lancaster Sound. After that no news was heard of them.

The years 1846, 1847, and 1848 passed without a word from Franklin and his men. Friends and relatives in England grew anxious and the government sent out no less than twenty-one expeditions hoping to find traces of the lost explorers. A reward of £20,000 for news of Franklin was offered by the Government and to this Lady Franklin added another £3,000. All of the expeditions returned without news. Lady Franklin, however, did not give up hope for she believed that her husband might still be alive. She outfitted a small yacht, the *Fox,* under the command of Captain McClintock for a search. McClintock and most of the crew willingly gave their services free. They were determined to solved the mystery of Franklin's fate if it was at all possible.

The *Fox* sailed to Greenland and was forced to winter there but as soon as the ice began to melt, it pushed on across Baffin Bay to Lancaster Sound. The second winter was spent near Boothia Peninsula. In spring, sledge parties which were sent out brought back important news. On the shore they had found the graves of three sailors, members of Franklin's expedition. From the Eskimos they had learned that the white men had passed that way many months before. In a village, not far away, McClintock's men found knives, buttons and silver spoons which had belonged to Franklin's men. The rescue party pushed on without delay.

From an old Eskimo they learned that far down to the south, off King William's Land, a great ship had been crushed in the ice. The Eskimo stated that it was a dangerous journey to this spot. At once preparations were were made for the long sledge journey.

Many weeks later the band of men reached an Eskimo village where they found the natives using guns, telescopes, forks, and spoons belonging to Franklin. From the Eskimos they learned that both the *Erebus* and *Terror* had been found crushed in the ice not far away and that many of the party had perished. Those few white men who remained alive had set out for the mainland.

THEY FOUND A TORN PIECE OF PAPER

Pushing on, McClintock and his men came upon the most important discovery of all. Beneath a pile of stones, they found a ragged, torn piece of paper, placed there by Franklin himself, telling some of the story of the ill-fated expedition. It told of the voyage through Lancaster Sound, of the two long dreary winters spent in the frozen Arctic, near King William's Land and of Franklin's plan with the coming of spring to push on through the ice-packs to the Pacific. Later the cairn of stones had been re-opened and around the edges and on the back of the paper more notes had been added telling of the tragic death of Sir John Franklin and of nine officers and fourteen of the men. It told of their plan to leave the helpless ships and to travel by sledge over the ice to the mainland for help at some Eskimo settlement. In one corner of the tattered paper was the last entry of all: "And start to-morrow for Back's Fish River."

This last message gave McClintock the information he wanted. He set out in the direction of the river but he did not reach it. On the way there he found, mounted on a sledge, a boat with two bodies in it. He found, too, watches, clothes and other belongings of the party as well as a Bible and a prayer book. Nearby in the snow lay the gaunt skeleton of the last of the party. From an old Eskimo, McClintock learned of this man's death. "He fell down and died as he walked." All of the ship's company, one hundred and thirty men had perished in the desolate Arctic wastes.

Franklin and his men had found the North-west Passage through Lancaster Sound at the price of their lives. In Westminster Abbey a beautiful monument was unveiled to Franklin's memory. On it were carved these words written by Lord Tennyson, Franklin's nephew.

Not here, the white North hath thy bones, and thou,
Heroic Sailor Soul,
Art passing on thy happier voyage now
Towards no earthly Pole.

TEST

Which of the following statements are true, and which false?

1. Franklin made seven journeys in search of a North-west Passage.
2. In the northern part of Canada Franklin found many lakes and rivers.
3. On his first journey to the Arctic Franklin travelled along the coast by canoe.
4. On this journey he and his men suffered from lack of food.

5. Later, on a second trip, Franklin journeyed down the Mackenzie River to the Arctic Ocean.
6. Along the coast of the Arctic Ocean, Franklin found no Eskimo settlements.
7. On his last journey Franklin's two ships were the *Sunshine* and the *Moonshine*.
8. When no news was heard from Franklin for fifteen years, the British government sent search parties to try to find him.
9. Captain McClintock found out that Franklin and many of his men had perished on King William's Land.
10. Without actually knowing it, Franklin had found the Northwest Passage.

THINGS TO DO

1. Pretend that you are Franklin and that you have come back to this world to look at the Arctic of the present day. What changes would you see?
2. Eskimos live in the Arctic region. What food do they eat? What clothes do they wear? Why have they healthy teeth?
3. Make models of the water craft and homes used, (1) by Eskimos, and (2) by North American Indians.
4. On a map of Canada mark in the routes taken by Franklin on his journeys. Use a different coloured crayon for each route. Print the names of the following places on your map: (1) Hudson Bay, (2) Coppermine River, (3) Arctic Ocean, (4) Point Turnagain, (5) Great Bear Lake, (6) Mackenzie River, (7) Lancaster Sound, (8) King William's Land.

BOOKS TO READ

For the Teacher
The Book of the Long Trail, H. Newbolt. *Longmans Green & Co.*
Exploration and Discovery, A. Archer. *Cambridge University Press.*
Great Navigators and Discoverers, J. A. Brendon. *George G. Harrap & Co. Ltd.*

For the Pupil

A Book of Discovery, M. B. Synge. *Thomas Nelson & Sons.*
The Book of Discovery, T. C. Bridges. *George G. Harrap & Co. Ltd.*
The Book of Polar Exploration, E. L. Elias. *George G. Harrap & Co. Ltd.*
Heroes of Exploration, R. Finch. *University of London Press.*

"THE POLE AT LAST!"

VII. TO THE ENDS OF THE EARTH

ADMIRAL PEARY AT THE NORTH POLE

FOR over twenty-three years Robert Peary, an American explorer, had been sailing to the Arctic, hoping to reach the North Pole; but each expedition had failed. On these voyages however he had learned many things: that Greenland is an island; that white men can exist in the Arctic for long months at a time if they live like the Eskimos; that Eskimo dogs are of great value in pulling heavy loads of supplies, and saving the strength of the men.

On July 6, 1909, Peary, then fifty-three years of age, set out on what he hoped would prove to be his last voyage to the north. He planned on this expedition to reach the North Pole. His ship, the *Roosevelt,* was made of sturdy oak. Never before had a ship been so well built for sailing

TREASURE

through the dangerous ice-fields. Her sides were two feet thick. If caught in an ice-pack, she would be able to rise above it rather than have her sides crushed in by the tremendous pressure of the ice. Her captain, Bob Bartlett, a Newfoundlander, was an experienced explorer and navigator. He had accompanied Peary on many other trips and knew the Arctic seas better, perhaps, than any man of his time. Another man on board was Matt Henson, a Negro, who was Peary's servant and closest friend; he had accompanied his master on all of his previous trips to the north. Many people said that Matt Henson knew as much about the Arctic as Peary did himself.

The *Roosevelt* steamed northward through the Atlantic Ocean to Etah, an Eskimo village on the western shores of Greenland. At this place Peary was well known for he had been here on twenty other trips. Eskimos in their kayaks paddled out to welcome him. When they learned of his plans, they begged to go with their friend. Natives who were good hunters and sledge-drivers and certain women specially skilled in the making of fur garments were chosen and allowed to join the ship. Over two hundred and forty-five tough Eskimo dogs were also brought on board; these were to be used to pull the heavy sledges during the long journey ahead. Stores of fishing-lines, harness, kayaks, harpoons and sledges were brought along and these filled the deck space.

The vessel then journeyed westward across the ice-filled waters till Grant Land was reached. Peary believed that this was the closest land to the North Pole and it was here that he planned to spend the winter before making his final dash to the Pole.

When the ice closed in around the ship, Peary was forced to establish winter quarters at a place on the coast of Grant Land which he named Cape Sheridan. Supplies were unloaded and, in a short time, a little village grew up. The Eskimo dogs scampered about joyfully in the snow so happy were they to be free once again. Eskimo men set to work to hunt fresh meat, polar bear, deer and musk-oxen, while the Eskimo women busied themselves sewing. Parties of men, with sledges piled high with supplies, set out overland for the most northerly point on the island. At this new camp, which they named Cape Columbia, they stored vast quantities of provisions of all kinds. All parties were back at Cape Sheridan in time for Christmas which was celebrated by feasting and racing in the snow.

During the long Arctic winter, Peary and his party completed their arrangements for the journey to the Pole, which they planned to make early in March when the sun re-

PEARY'S JOURNEY TO THE
NORTH POLE

turned. They knew the dangers that lay ahead and they were determined that nothing should go wrong. This time of waiting was trying for both white men and Eskimos.

Late in February, Peary with a party of white men and Eskimos left Cape Sheridan and set out by sledge for Cape Columbia. When they had settled down in this new camp, a party of men under Bob Bartlett was sent on ahead over the frozen sea to cut through the ridges of ice and make the road easier for the rest of the party which was to follow shortly. When Peary finally set out there were seven white men, Matt Henson, and fifty-nine Eskimos with him as well as one hundred and forty dogs and twenty-eight sledges. The journey northward was a grim one. Often wide lanes of water would suddenly open up in the ice and the men would be forced to wait for days till the sea froze over again. Sometimes they had to climb over huge bergs held fast in the ice; some of these rose to heights of over one hundred feet. Often the temperature went down to sixty degrees below zero. Every few days Peary checked the party and sent the weakest men and dogs back to Cape Columbia. After the day's march was over, the men rested. No tents were set up but Eskimo igloos were built, for Peary knew that they would stand up well against the driving winds and that they would still be standing and provide shelter for the explorers when they returned from the north. In these igloos, supplies of food were stored.

When the party was about one hundred and thirty-two miles from the Pole, Peary chose Matt Henson and four sturdy Eskimos to accompany him on the final dash; all of the other men were sent back to the base camp. Peary also selected forty Eskimo dogs to pull the five sledges which carried enough food to last them for forty days.

Now the explorers were on the last lap of the journey. Luckily, the ice became smoother and the weather improved. Each day they were able to travel well over the thirty miles. At six each morning they rose, ate a light breakfast and travelled until three in the afternoon when they stopped and had mugs of steaming hot tea and ships' biscuits. In late afternoon, the camp was set up. The Eskimos built an igloo while Peary and Henson prepared supper. This meal consisted of pemmican (dried beef mixed with currants, raisins, cocoa, suet and sugar), ships' biscuits and hot tea. When the dogs had been fed they curled up in the snow for the night while the men, inside the igloo, crept into their sleeping-bags.

One morning an accident occurred in which Matt Henson nearly lost his life. As he was crossing some newly-formed ice he, his dogs, and his sledge suddenly plunged into the frigid waters of the Arctic Ocean. Henson's heavy clothes nearly pulled him under and it was only after a tremendous struggle that he managed to reach safety. When he was rescued, his clothes were stiff with ice and he was nearly frozen to death. The Eskimos, well used to such accidents, beat the ice out of his clothes and Peary poured hot drinks down Henson's throat. Henson recovered and suffered no ill effects from his icy bath. The sledge and dogs too had been pulled safely to firm ice.

On the sixth of April, Robert Peary reached the North Pole. A silken flag, the Stars and Stripes, which had been made by his wife and which he had worn wrapped around his body during each previous journey was proudly hoisted. Peary wrote in his diary these words: "The Pole at last! The prize of over three centuries! My dream and goal for twenty years—mine at last! I cannot bring myself to realize it." Peary found that there is no land at the North Pole, only ice, and below the ice the dark cold waters of the ocean. The party spent about thirty hours at the Pole. Although they built an igloo and prepared for a rest they were unable to sleep; they were far too excited to remain quiet.

Before leaving Peary wrote a postcard to his wife and this is what he said:

90 degrees North Latitude,
Apr. 7, 1909.

My dear Jo,—

I have won at last. Have been here a day. I start for home in an hour. Love to the kiddies.

Bob.

Peary carried this card with him to the south and posted it at the first post-office he reached on the homeward voyage. It arrived in New York long before he did himself.

The journey to the North Pole from Cape Columbia had taken thirty-seven days but the return journey took only sixteen, for the weather was ideal and travel was much easier. Peary was glad to be able to hurry back for he feared that if warmer weather set in, the ice might break and cut off his return to camp. On April 23, the party reached camp, weary and tired, but none the worse for the journey and happy at their success.

TEST

In sentences, write answers to the following questions:
1. Who was Peary?
2. Why did he sail?
3. Why was the *Roosevelt* a suitable ship in which to travel in the Arctic seas?
4. What supplies did Peary obtain from the Eskimos at Etah, Greenland?
5. Why were certain Eskimo women chosen to accompany Peary's party of explorers?
6. What Arctic animals provided fresh meat for the party?
7. What is pemmican?
8. Why did Peary and his men sleep in igloos instead of tents?
9. Who were with Peary when he reached his goal?
10. On what date did he reach his goal?

THINGS TO DO

1. Make your own map of the Arctic region and on it show Peary's route on his journey to the Pole. On it mark in the following places: Greenland, Etah, Davis Strait, Grant Land, Cape Sheridan, Cape Columbia, North Pole.
2. Make a sketch of the flag Peary planted at the Pole. What do we call this flag?
3. Make a table scene to show Peary's winter camp at Cape Sheridan. Remember to include the following in your scene: igloos, husky dogs, sledges, kayaks, seals and Eskimos.
4. Get pictures of the kinds of animals that Peary probably saw in the Arctic. Write a sentence under each picture describing the animal. Put these pictures on your class bulletin board.

BOOKS TO READ

For the Teacher

Exploration and Discovery, A. B. Archer. *Cambridge University Press*.

Unrolling the Map, Leonard Outhwaite. *McClelland and Stewart*.

For the Pupil

The Book of Discovery, T. C. Bridges. *George G. Harrap & Co. Ltd.*

A Book of Discovery, M. B. Synge. *Thos. Nelson & Sons Limited*.

The Book of Polar Exploration, E. L. Elias. *George G. Harrap & Co. Ltd.*

Boys' Book of Exploration, M. Harris Gable. *E. P. Dutton & Co.*

Heroes of Discovery, R. Finch. *University of London Press*.

They Went Exploring, Arensa Sondergaard. *Harper & Bros.*

The Top of the World, A. Gall & F. Crew. *Oxford University Press*.

THE QUEST FOR THE SOUTH POLE

SHACKLETON

Many explorers believed that a great southern continent lay far to the south of Australia but no man was certain for none had ever set foot on it. Many times Captain James Cook had attempted to sail through the Antarctic seas and reach land but each time he had been forced back by the great masses of floating ice.

In 1901 an expedition was planned by a group of Englishmen and Captain Robert Scott was chosen to command it. His ship, the *Discovery,* had been especially built for this voyage. It was of oak and the ship-builders said that it would withstand the tremendous pressure of the ice-pack much better than a ship of steel. On board the *Discovery* was a crew of forty men, all experienced sailors, volunteers from the Royal Navy. One of the junior officers was Ernest Shackleton, who had already made many voyages to distant places, to Cape Horn at the tip of South America, to the Cape of Good Hope, to India, and to the China coast. Shackleton had been chosen by Scott "mainly because of his knowledge of sails."

Leaving England the *Discovery* steamed south through the waters of the Atlantic, rounded the Cape of Good Hope and reached New Zealand after a voyage of many months. From New Zealand she headed for the Southern Seas. As she continued south, she met masses of floating ice; then in the distance the Great Ice Barrier was sighted, a huge wall of ice which surrounds all of the Antarctic continent. Scott was anxious to make a landing but, although he searched for many days along the edge of this high cliff of ice, no suitable place could be found. The great white barrier rose steeply from the water, towering in some places to a height of sixty feet. At last a little bay was sighted and here a successful landing was made. The men were thankful to be able to leave the ship and walk about on solid ice. The husky dogs and ponies frolicked about over the ice and snow, glad once more to have their freedom after the cramped quarters aboard the *Discovery*. Days were spent unloading the supplies and in a week's time a camp was set up, the first in this snow-bound Antarctic region. Near their camp towered two great snow-clad mountains which afterwards were named Erebus and Terror. Mount Erebus, an active volcano, continually poured smoke and ashes high up into the air and the snow around the camp was covered with a fine grey dust. To the place where Scott set up his base camp, he gave the name King Edward VII Land in honour of the King of England.

During the winter months of darkness the party spent much time in their cosy winter quarters reading, making reports on weather conditions, and planning for the time when the sun would return once more. Many short trips from the camp were made into the neighbouring district. At one time Shackleton went up in a balloon and viewed this land from the air. He reported that it was a vast sheet of ice and snow as far as the eye could see with high mountains stretching far to the south.

That winter was a long dreary time; in the Antarctic the sun disappears early in April and does not return till late in August. Blizzards lasting many days at a time blew fiercely; great drifts of snow piled up around the hut and the temperature was far below zero all of the time.

As soon as the sun returned, Scott planned to set out on a journey which he hoped would take him to the South Pole. With him he planned to take Shackleton and Dr. Wilson, another member of the party. Food and supplies of clothing and fuel were carefully packed on three sledges, nineteen husky dogs were hitched up and, when all was ready, the party bade farewell to their comrades.

The heavy snow and the rough surface of the ice proved too much for the dogs. One after another they fell ill and died. This was a great hardship, for now the men were forced to pull the heavily-loaded sleds. As the days passed by, the strain grew greater as the surface of the snow grew rougher and travel was much more difficult. Often great cracks, called crevasses, appeared like great yawning mouths in the snow. The men were forced to stop and make bridges over the gaps or as was more often the case to detour many miles out of their way around these great cracks.

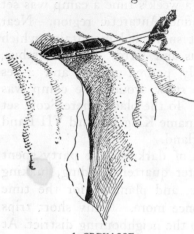

A CREVASSE

Christmas Day arrived and was celebrated while the men were on the trail. The Union Jack was flown over their tent and photographs were taken of each man standing beside this "little bit of England." Dinner was a very simple meal but Shackleton produced a great surprise which he had kept a secret up to this time. He had saved a tiny Christmas pudding, less than half a pound in weight, for this occasion. The pudding was heated in cocoa and divided carefully into helpings. What a treat it proved to be! "It was a glorious surprise to them—that plum pudding—when I produced it," Shackleton wrote in his diary.

Next morning they pushed on to the south. The farther they journeyed, the more their hardships increased. Cold bitter weather set in, fingers and toes were frost-bitten. The men were growing very weak from hunger, for food was very scarce. Each day they wondered how much farther they could go. One evening they came to a great deep crevasse, wider than any other they had yet seen and beyond it towered a steep cliff of ice. The way ahead was barred. Weary and tired the men crept into their sleeping bags to rest while they talked over what they should do. They knew they were over four hundred miles from the South Pole. They knew too that they had only enough food for thirteen days. In their hearts they realized that there was only one thing to do while they still had strength. They decided to return to the base camp.

All three were able to get back safely although they suffered hardships on the way. They had failed to reach their goal, the South Pole, but they had made the first long land journey ever made by men on the Antarctic continent.

SHACKLETON'S SECOND VOYAGE

Six years later Shackleton again set out for the Antarctic but this time he was in full command. His ship, the *Nimrod,* carried besides the crew, fifteen hardy little Manchurian ponies and nine Siberian sledge dogs. Many explorers in the polar regions favoured the use of dogs but Shackleton pinned his faith more on ponies. He felt that they were much stronger than the dogs; that they could pull heavier sledge loads, and were far easier to manage. If his men were faced with starvation, Shackleton knew that the ponies would provide food for the party. On board his ship were stores and supplies for two years, sledges built in Norway, and sleeping bags of reindeer skin. On the deck was something new to be tried out—a motor-sledge. Although Shackleton doubted whether it would be of much help in the heavy snow he had promised to give it at least a fair trial.

This time, as before, the party headed through the waters of the Antarctic till they came to the little bay at the foot of Mount Erebus where Scott's camp had stood. Getting the stores and dogs ashore was not difficult but the motor-sledge proved to be quite a trial for the men. Worst of all, however, were the ponies, for they had to be put in horse-boxes and hoisted up from the deck of the ship and then down to the ice. Once on the snow they were happy, and began to paw the surface snow and whinny, thinking no doubt that they were back home in North China. When everything was unloaded, Shackleton and his men set to work to build a winter camp.

The hut which was their winter quarters was spacious and comfortable. Often during the cold winter months when great blizzards raged and stormy winds shrieked around the walls of the hut, it shook and trembled but it never collapsed nor was it blown away. The men were busy exercising and feeding the ponies, carrying food to little storage bases and doing the hundred and one tasks that are necessary around such a camp. For a time, Shackleton made many efforts to use the motor-sledge but it proved a failure. The engine would not start in the zero temperatures. That winter the men saw a beautiful sight, the Southern Lights, similar to our Northern Lights, which lit up the sky with their many-coloured, ever-changing shafts of light.

Early in October, Shackleton and three of his most trusted men set out on the journey to the Pole with sledges, ponies and food supplies to last them for three months. Unfortunately their route lay through a mountainous part of the country and the ponies soon showed that they were not able to stand the strain of travel. Three of the little creatures grew so ill that they had to be shot. Each day the weather grew colder, blizzards raged, and snow fell continually. Before long all but one of the ponies had died from exhaustion. The survivor, a great favourite named Socks, carried on. One morning, Shackleton heard a cry of terror from the pony and, turning around, he saw little Socks slipping down into a deep crevasse. The pony's sledge was hanging over the edge of the great yawning hole. Everything was done to rescue Socks but it proved impossible. With sad hearts, the men continued on their way.

Unfortunately the ponies had died at a time when they were most needed, for the party had just begun to climb the steep side of a great hill of ice, the Beardmore Glacier. The work of pulling the heavy loads now fell to the men. By Christmas they had reached the top of the glacier. Before them to the south spread a great high plain. They knew that they were not far from the South Pole but the journey thus far had taken longer than they had planned and food supplies were nearly all used up. Only a month's supply of food was left. It was clear that unless they soon turned back they would perish in the snow. Leaving the heavy sledges behind, Shackleton and his men made a final effort to reach the Pole and they pushed on for a few more miles as far south as they could go. A flag which Queen Alexandra had given to Shackleton was planted, ninety-seven miles from the Pole. Before them, somewhere not far away to the south lay their goal, but this time, as before, they had failed to reach it. Sick with disappointment, Shackleton wrote in his diary: "Whatever our regret may be, we have done our best."

The homeward journey was a long terrible one for the men who were tired, hungry, and weak. It was as much as they could do to drag themselves on through the deep drifts of snow. Nearly every day some accident befell a member of the party. Finally, after days of trials which brought them very close to death, they reached the base camp.

THIRD VOYAGE

Years passed by. In that time other explorers sailed to the Antarctic. In 1911, Amundsen the great Norwegian explorer, successfully reached the South Pole and one month later the Englishman, Capt. Robert Scott, was also successful in reaching the Pole. More was now known about the Antarctic but, for the explorers, there was still much to learn.

Shackleton heard the call of the Antarctic once more and in 1914, after many months of preparation, he was ready to sail south. This time his plan was to cross Antarctica from sea to sea. Aboard his ship, the *Endurance,* Shackleton was wished every success by the king, George V. Then the *Endurance* sailed for the Atlantic.

The shores of South America were sighted and then the vessel headed for the rock-bound island of South Georgia. This British island which is one of the loneliest and most desolate of places has for many years been used as a base in the whaling industry and is the furthest point to the south where people live. From South Georgia, the *Endurance* headed south again, crossed the Antarctic Circle and entered the iceberg zone which surrounds the great frozen wastes of Antarctica. In a single day Shackleton's men counted no less than five hundred icebergs, many of them coming far too near the ship for safety. The *Endurance* then reached the ice-pack which reaches out from the Great Ice Barrier. She made her perilous way through it looking for a suitable landing place. None could be found. The great chunks of ice closed in around the ship and held her fast in their grip. As the hours passed by the ice continued to press against the sides of the *Endurance* and before long Shackleton knew that his ship would be crushed. With a heavy heart he gave orders to abandon ship. Provisions, clothing, fuel, and small boats were quickly unloaded and

GREAT CAKES OF ICE CRUSHED THE SHIP

carried to a flat sheet of ice near the ship. Then the men watched the great cakes of ice press and crush the sides of the doomed ship as if they were frail pieces of matchwood. Before their eyes the *Endurance* was sucked under into the icy seas and disappeared.

Their plight was serious. Spring was coming and they knew that the great sheet of ice on which they had placed their precious stores would soon break up into pieces. Then the pieces would drift out to sea. Soon, as though in warning, cracks began to appear. Hastily the men rescued their supplies and scrambled to a safer place but they knew that, before long, they would be forced to take to the small boats. The wind and current were both against them for they were taking the ice farther and farther out to sea, and farther and farther away from the Great Ice Barrier. Launching the small boats, the men put out to sea. After days adrift, they reached the shores of Elephant Island, a steep, rocky mountain top rising up above the storm-swept sea. The twenty-two half-frozen survivors crouched under their overturned rowboat and discussed what they should do next. They were at least eight hundred miles from South Georgia the nearest island where help could be obtained. Shackleton knew that some of the party would have to face the voyage to South Georgia. It was their only chance; otherwise he and his men would be faced with starvation and death on the lonely island.

Shackleton and six others volunteered to make the trip. They set out in one of the rowboats, the *James Baird*, on one of the most daring journeys ever attempted by men. As they left the shores of Elephant Island, they waved farewell to their comrades on shore and wondered if they would ever meet again. A fierce wind came up and, for fourteen days, a hurricane blew. Sleet and spray formed into ice, covering everything in the boat. With this thick icy layer the boat grew so heavy that it nearly sank. With freezing fingers, the men crawled about and chopped as much ice as they could from the boat and its equipment. They placed a covering over the bow of the boat and in its shelter, in turns, took a few hours of rest, protected from the lashing of the icy waves. A mast and sail were also rigged up. Ice covered the men from head to feet and their hands and feet were severely frost-bitten. In spite of all these hardships, they never once gave up hope. Finally they reached their goal, South Georgia. Unfortunately Shackleton had reached the opposite side of the island from that on which the little

TO THE ENDS OF THE EARTH 199

whaling village was located. He made several attempts to land but every time he was driven back by high waves and rocks along the shores. Shackleton was fearful that he and his party might perish so close to help. At last a landing was made and after a thirty-six hour march through steep mountain passes the little village was reached. Some boys who were playing near the settlement were the first to see the ghostly-looking men staggering towards them. Frightened by the men's appearance, the children fled to tell their parents. The kind folk did all that could be done to help Shackleton and his men, giving them warm clothes, hot drinks, food, and comfortable beds.

Several weeks passed before a suitable rescue boat could be secured. Shackleton feared that in the meantime many of the men marooned on the island might have died of the cold and from starvation. When at last help was obtained and they neared the shores of Elephant Island, Shackleton called out, "Are you all well?" To his great joy voices answered, "All safe, all well." Through the days of waiting the men had remained confident that Shackleton would return for them. Each morning the leader had cheerfully called out to his men, "Roll up your sleeping bags, boys; the boss (Shackleton) may come to-day." So thankful were they for their rescue from almost certain death that they decided to keep August 30, the day of their rescue, as a special festival day for the rest of their lives.

Fourth Voyage

In 1920, Shackleton, now a man of forty-seven years of age, started out on his fourth and last voyage to the Antarctic. His ship, the *Quest*, reached South Georgia after a journey of four months. During the voyage Shackleton who had been in poor health suffered from a severe attack of influenza. On his arrival at the whaling station his friends there gave him a warm welcome. They noticed how he had aged and how sickness had weakened him. After a dinner of welcome Shackleton returned that night to his ship to write his diary and to make final arrangements for his journey south. The voyage never took place. That night Shackleton suffered a sudden heart attack and died. When the news travelled to Britain all the country mourned for the great explorer and special services were held in St. Paul's Cathedral in London.

According to his wishes, Shackleton was buried amidst the snow and ice of South Georgia near Antarctica to which he had journeyed so often.

TEST

1. Why did Shackleton go to Antarctica?
2. Shackleton took Manchurian ponies to pull the sledges over the snow in the Antarctic. Give two reasons why he preferred ponies to husky dogs.
3. What are crevasses? Why were they feared by explorers?
4. What is a blizzard?
5. How long does the "Antarctic night" last?
6. Why did Shackleton and his party fail to reach Antarctica on the third voyage?
7. Why was the voyage from Elephant Island to South Georgia a terrible one?
8. When Shackleton and his men reached South Georgia on the third expedition why did the children from the village run away from them?
9. Why did Shackleton wish to be buried in South Georgia?
10. Of what value to Britain is the island of South Georgia to-day?

THINGS TO DO

1. With your crayons or coloured chalk draw pictures on a long sheet of wrapping paper to show scenes from Shackleton's four voyages. Here are some ideas (*a*) Shackleton's ship making its way through the Antarctic icebergs. (*b*) The base camp near Mount Erebus. (*c*) The journey from Elephant Island to South Georgia. (*d*) A sledge journey in Antarctica.
2. Why would you dislike spending a winter in Antarctica?
3. In your opinion why was Shackleton knighted by the King of England?
4. Shackleton sent to Manchuria for ponies before he started out on his second expedition. Describe the route these ponies must have taken in order to journey from Manchuria to Britain.

BOOKS TO READ

For the Teacher

A History of Geographical Discovery and Exploration, J. N. L. Baker. *George G. Harrap & Co. Ltd.*

For the Pupil

A Book of Discovery, M. B. Synge. *Thos. Nelson & Sons Limited.*

The Book of Discovery, T. C. Bridges. *George G. Harrap & Co. Ltd.*

The Book of Polar Exploration, E. L. Elias. *George G. Harrap & Co. Ltd.*

Boys' Book of Exploration, M. Harris Gable. *E. P. Dutton & Co.*

AMUNDSEN

When Roald Amundsen of Norway was a boy of fifteen
he had decided to be an Arctic explorer. He had read and
re-read stories of the great journeys into the north by men
like Sir John Franklin and Amunsden's fellow Norwegian,
Dr. Nansen, and he planned to follow in their footsteps and
explore the frozen wastes of the Arctic. In the meantime
he worked steadily at school, and after hours he learned all
that he could about seamanship and navigation.

The first journey he made was through the waters in
which Franklin had sailed. Amundsen was the first white
man to make the complete journey through the North-west
Passage from east to west.

His next journey was to have been an expedition to the
North Pole. Luckily he obtained a ship well-suited to
Arctic travel, Dr. Nansen's famous ship, the *Fram*. It had
been especially built for weathering the stormy waters of
the northern seas and for battling its way through the thick
ice-floes. Just as Amundsen was ready to set out the news
reached him that Admiral Robert Peary of the United
States had reached the North Pole. Amundsen decided
that he would journey to the Antarctic and make a dash
for the South Pole. His plan was kept secret, for Amundsen
knew that a British expedition commanded by Captain
Robert Scott had set out for the Antarctic one month before
this time.

Amundsen's party was a small one, but they were expert
skiers and were well trained to live in the extreme cold of
the polar regions. Every man was in perfect health. With
him, Amundsen had one hundred husky dogs to pull the
heavy loads, for he knew from past experience that dogs
could endure far greater hardships than the ponies which
Scott planned to use.

When Amundsen and his party arrived in the Antarctic, winter, which begins in April and lasts till early August, had set in. First, supplies were unloaded from the *Fram*, a comfortable hut was built, and the men settled down to make final plans for the long journey to the Pole. Some men were sent out on a seal hunt from which they returned with one

ALL OF THE PARTY WERE EXPERT SKIERS

hundred and twenty thousand pounds of seal flesh. This fresh meat was to do the men on the long journey ahead of them. It did much to help prevent scurvy. Amundsen afterwards stated that he had not had even one case of this disease during his entire stay in the Antarctic. Amundsen was at all times very anxious to keep his men in excellent health. He insisted that each one wear six pairs of heavy woollen stockings under his boots! As a result no man suffered from frost-bitten feet even though the temperature was often as low as seventy-four degrees below zero.

Like the British explorer, Scott, Amundsen sent out members of his party during the winter to establish depots, three in all, along the route to the Pole. All around these supply bases, for a distance of five miles, flags were placed to guide the men to the food and supplies when they returned from their journey to the South Pole. Many shelters were built along the route too, for Amundsen well knew that these would be needed when bitter driving blizzards blew across the frozen wastes. Everything possible was done so that the party would not suffer from the cold or run short of supplies on the journey.

Early in October, five men, four sledges, and fifty-two dogs set off. As the party advanced the men lightened their loads every few miles by setting up cairns and storing supplies of food and fuel; near each cairn a snow beacon six feet in height was set up to act as a guide to the party on their return. In all, one hundred and fifty of these snow beacons were built. Many dangers faced the men along the way, biting cold, driving blizzards, and great yawning crevasses. At times these cracks forced the men to make detours of many miles. One day a crack opened up beneath the feet of the dogs. Both dogs and sledge were hurled down and precious supplies were in danger of being lost. One man instantly volunteered to go down the steep side of the chasm to rescue the dogs and supplies. Using long ropes the supplies, sledge, and dogs were hoisted up to safety and soon all were ready to continue on the journey. Each day brought its own hardships but the men faced each new danger bravely.

By November they reached the high plateau which surrounds the South Pole. A furious blizzard raged for several days and during this time the party rested and gained strength for the final dash. Supplies of fresh meat were growing very low and Amundsen was forced to kill twenty-four of his dogs for food. To the place where his dogs were put to death Amundsen gave the name Butcher's Camp. The last week of the journey, the party covered over fifteen miles each day, for the weather was good all the way and at times the men even enjoyed bright sunshine which is unusual in the Antarctic region.

On December 14, 1911 Amundsen came within sight of his goal. He stared ahead, anxious to know if the British party had arrived before him. There were no signs of ski-tracks, no flags, no foot-prints in the snow. At three o'clock in the afternoon Amundsen reached the South Pole. He had won the race and had beaten Capt. Scott. A beautiful silk

THE NORWEGIAN FLAG WAS PLANTED ON THE SPOT

Norwegian flag was planted on the spot. Inside a cairn of stones Amundsen placed records of the journey, a letter to Scott and some food supplies. When the party had rested three days, the return journey was begun. Everything went well for the men; the weather was good and they had no trouble in finding the food depots which had been carefully marked. In record time, thirty-nine days, Amundsen and his men arrived back at their base camp on the Bay of Whales.

Amundsen had won. His success was due to many things: he had spent years living in the Arctic and was an experienced polar explorer; he and his men were skilled skiers; his dogs were a great help, they proved that they could endure the cold of the Antarctic and they provided food when it was needed; and, perhaps most important of all, he and his men were in excellent health during the entire trip. Of course he was fortunate in having, for the most part, good weather.

Some years later, in 1928, Amundsen lost his life in the Arctic. He had gone out by plane in charge of a party searching for the wrecked airship of an Italian explorer, General Nobile. The Italian airship was found by another rescue plane but no word was ever again heard from Amundsen.

TEST

Supply the missing words:

1. Early in life Amundsen decided to be an ————.
2. He was the first man to sail through the North-west Passage from ———— to ————.
3. Next he intended to journey to the ———— but he was forced to change his plans because ———— had reached there before Amundsen set out.
4. When Amundsen sailed to the Antarctic he kept his plans a ————because he knew that a ———— party was already on its way to that region.
5. Amundsen built his base camp in Antarctica near the Bay of ————.
6. Early in October he and ———— other men set out on a journey to the South Pole.
7. The party travelled on ———— and their heavily-loaded sledges were pulled by ————.
8. Amundsen planted the flag of ———— at the South Pole.
9. He arrived there on December ——, 19——.
10. On the return journey from the South Pole, Amundsen had no trouble finding supplies of food because they had been carefully marked by ————.

THINGS TO DO

1. Make a sketch of a sledge. Pack it with things which Amundsen would carry on this journey to the South Pole. Name each parcel.
2. Imagine that you are Amundsen. What do you think he wrote in his diary when he reached the South Pole?
3. How did Amundsen dress? What did he eat?
4. Make a sketch showing Amundsen at the South Pole.
5. Choose one pupil to read and tell the class the story of Amundsen's journey through the North-west Passage.

BOOKS TO READ

FOR THE TEACHER

Unrolling the Map, Leonard Outhwaite. *McClelland & Stewart.*

FOR THE PUPIL

A Book of Discovery, M. B. Synge. *Thos. Nelson & Sons Limited.*

The Book of Discovery, T. C. Bridges. *George G. Harrap & Co. Ltd.*

The Book of Polar Exploration, E. L. Elias. *George G. Harrap & Co. Ltd.*

Boys' Book of Exploration, J. Harris Gable. *E. P. Dutton & Co.*

Explorers All, B. Anthony and M. Barnes. *The Fideler Company, Grand Rapids, Mich.*

Map Makers, J. Cottler and H. Jaffe. *The Ryerson Press.*

SCOTT

Britain had become interested in the Antarctic region. Captain Robert Scott, an experienced explorer and seaman who had already headed an expedition to the South Pole, was chosen to head another. After long months of preparation, Scott's ship, the *Terra Nova*, was ready to sail. On board with Scott were sixty officers, scientists, and seamen. No expense had been spared in fitting out the sturdy vessel and it carried in its hold supplies of food, clothing, and fuel for over three years.

The vessel journeyed southward through the Atlantic and on east around the Cape of Good Hope till the shores of New Zealand came into view. Here supplies of food and fuel were taken on board and when all was ready the *Terra Nova* sailed out from the harbour at Lyttleton amidst the screaming of sirens and the cheering of crowds of people bidding farewell to the explorers.

All went well until the third day out, when a fierce gale blew up and roared across the decks, while mountainous waves swept over the ship. Scott feared for his ship and precious cargo and for the safety of his men. All hands were quickly called up to help to pump the rising water out of the hold. After twenty-four hours of terror the seas grew calm and the danger passed. Much damage had been done to the ship however, and two ponies and one husky dog had died during the storm. As they voyaged south, the weather grew colder, snow fell, and the *Terra Nova* was covered with a thick sheet of ice. Great icebergs, towering high above the ship, floated dangerously close to her bow. After nosing her way through great fields of floating ice she came, at last, to the Great Ice Barrier which surrounds the Antarctic continent. For days, Scott searched along the barrier for a suitable place to land but found none. Near the great Antarctic volcano named Erebus, Scott sighted a little bay and headed his ship into it. Here he found a landing-place. Supplies were unloaded with great difficulty and a base camp was set up. In less than a week, the men had everything they needed ashore and they had also built a comfortable hut which was to be their home during the cold winter which lay ahead. Tons of supplies were checked over and piled up near the hut, and shelters were built for the animals. Scott had brought with him nineteen Siberian ponies and thirty-four husky dogs. He favoured the use of the ponies, for a pony could pull a sledge loaded with six hundred and fifty pounds while many dogs were needed to pull the same load. He had also brought along three motor-sledges, which were a new mode of travel and in which he had no great faith.

On the Antarctic continent, it is so cold that few animals are found there. The only living creatures that Scott's men found were penguins on land and seals and whales in the icy seas. Each day hundreds of these friendly little penguins waddled about near the camp looking like little gentlemen in frock coats and white vests. In his diary Scott wrote that they seemed to say, "Halloa! what do all you ridiculous things want?" These little creatures and the seals provided the party with their only supply of fresh meat during their stay in the Antarctic.

Scott planned to store food and fuel at certain places along the route to the South Pole. Parties of men with teams of dogs or ponies harnessed to sledges transported tons of provisions to the storehouses, which they set up every few miles along the route. Two of the largest depots were named Corner Camp and One-ton Depot. The work of the men was far from easy for they suffered greatly from the cold and were very often delayed by bad weather. Heavy falls of snow and stinging blizzards often delayed parties for many days. During these times the men set up tents and rested and slept in their sleeping bags till the weather cleared. The dogs curled up in the snow and kept warm in snug little holes, but the ponies, without suitable shelters to protect them from the biting winds and furious blizzards, sickened and died.

One day as Scott and his men were taking supplies to a depot, an accident occurred which nearly ended in disaster for a team of the dogs. Scott was walking beside a sledge when the team of thirteen dogs suddenly disappeared down a crevasse. Quickly anchoring the sledge in the snow, Scott climbed down into the deep chasm and managed to haul all of the dogs but two to safety. The two lay, badly hurt, on a snowy bridge, sixty feet below the surface. Climbing down to the lower level, Scott fastened the helpless creatures in nets and they were pulled up to safety. Later, when Scott reached the surface, his men found that both of their leader's hands had been badly frost-bitten. Scott had not thought of himself; his only concern had been for the safety of his dogs.

When winter set in, the members of the party returned to camp and prepared for the dash to the Pole. One group of men studied the Emperor penguins and their habits, another group was put in charge of caring for the ponies and dogs. All of the men worked happily together. They published a newspaper which they named the *South Polar Times*. Much of their free time was spent reading, singing, and playing cards. Their light was provided by candles or blubber lamps. Scott said in his diary that he had never before been with such a fine, happy group of men. Thus the long weeks of darkness passed and by August the sun shone once more.

By November everything was ready for the dash to the Pole. For a few days the motor sledges were used but the

Antarctic cold was too much for them; the engines over-heated and the sledges gave so much trouble that they had to be left behind. Scott had pinned his hopes on the ponies. They proved unable to withstand the cold and one by one they had to be killed. Finally the party was left with only two dog teams. The rest of the supplies had to be pulled on sledges by the men. In spite of difficulties the men were able to cover over fifteen miles every day.

Early in December the party reached the great Beardmore Glacier, and the difficult climb up its steep side began. Bad weather held them back, for

SCOTT'S ROUTE TO THE SOUTH POLE

a blizzard blew up and continued for many days. The runners of the two sledges became coated with ice and little headway was made up the slippery steep surface. The blizzard was followed by a snowstorm which formed deep drifts and these helped the men, for they were now able to use skis. When December 25 arrived, Scott proclaimed a holiday. Christmas Day was a happy time. The men ate pemmican, pony meat, chocolate, plum pudding, cocoa, ginger, and caramels and they sang carols. Next day after this short rest they continued on their way. By the end of the month the summit of the great glacier was reached and a high flat plateau lay before them.

They were now eight hundred miles from their base camp. Because food supplies were running low, Scott decided to choose four of the healthiest, strongest men to remain with him on the final dash to the South Pole while the others were to be sent back with the dogs to camp. The month's supply of food which they took with them on the sledges had to be pulled by the men themselves. Dr. Wilson, Bowers, Capt. Oates, Petty Officer Evans, and Scott made up the party of five. Just before setting out, Scott wrote these words. "I am going forward with a party of five men with a month's provisions, and the prospect of success seems good, provided the weather holds and no unforeseen obstacles arise."

Although they only had a distance of one hundred and forty-five miles to go to the Pole, most of it on flat ground, the journey proved to be a terrible one. A blizzard which blew for over twenty-four hours delayed them and after that came five days of appalling cold. It was impossible to keep toes and fingers from freezing. The men were only able to travel about ten miles each day.

By the middle of January only twenty miles remained between Scott and the Pole and on that day Scott wrote these words in his diary: "It is wonderful to think that two long marches will land us at the Pole. Only twenty miles from the Pole—we ought to do it now."

Next day brought a bitter disappointment. One of the men saw in the distance a black speck. When they drew nearer they found it to be a flag tied to a sledge. Close by,

Scott found the remains of a camp and marks in the snow of skis, dogs, and sledge tracks. Scott had heard, before he set out from the base camp, that a group of Norwegians commanded by Amundsen were in the Antarctic to make a dash for the South Pole. He knew now that someone had reached the Pole ahead of him.

On January 17, 1912, Scott found a cairn over which flew the flag of Norway and in the cairn he found a record which stated that Capt. Amundsen and his party had reached the South Pole. They had been there one month earlier, in the middle of December. This was a terrible blow to Scott and to all of the party.

The South Pole was found to be on a high snow-covered plain. At the Pole, Scott hoisted a silk Union Jack, a gift from Queen Alexandra, which he had carried wrapped around his body. Under a cairn of stones, Scott left a record, showing that the British party had reached their goal. Photographs were taken and then the men prepared to face the long journey back to camp.

That night they slept very little. They had much to worry them. Food supplies were low, they were tired and they were bitterly disappointed. They knew, too, that they were facing a long and difficult journey. Scott showed that he was very uneasy for, in his diary, he wrote these words: "Now for the run home and a desperate struggle. I wonder if we can do it."

In this frame of mind they began their march back. Bad luck followed them every mile. The weather which had been bad grew worse. At first they were able to find the stones marking the food depots without much difficulty, but as the gales and snow increased, they could not locate the markers. Without sufficient food the men grew weaker; every bone in their bodies ached. At last they reached the edge of the Beardmore Glacier. Before them lay the journey down hill but the surface was covered with polished glistening ice and each step of the way was full of danger.

Petty Officer Evans, who up until this time had been the strongest man in the party, fell and received a serious head injury; he was also suffering from severe frost-bite of the hands and nose. During the following week he grew much worse and Scott decided to rest for a few days and care for Evans. The weary men set up a camp in the shelter of a great cliff of sandstone. Evans was sinking fast and on February 17 he died. His loss was felt keenly by the others. With heavy hearts they buried their comrade and struggled on over the Great Ice Barrier. In a few days they reached a food depot but in it they found no fuel. This was serious; in the low temperatures of the Antarctic it is impossible to keep well without one hot meal every day.

The cold became more intense and the surface of the snow was rougher and more difficult for travel. By the middle of March, the four men were losing count of the days. A furious blizzard began to blow and continued for several days. The men set up their tent and remained huddled in their sleeping bags. Captain Oates had for some time been very ill, but he had not uttered one word of complaint. He knew that his illness would hold the others back when the storm was over; he also knew that they would not go on and leave him to die alone. He did what is one of the most heroic acts ever recorded. Turning to Scott, he said, "I am just going outside and may be some time." He walked out into the raging blizzard and was never seen again. "We knew," wrote Scott, "that poor Oates was walking to his death but though we tried to dissuade him we knew that it was the act of a brave man and an English gentleman."

Dragging themselves along as best they could, the three men struggled on. On March 29, they made their last camp.

Another blizzard, worse than the last, howled around their tiny tent. Inside huddled the three survivors. They had only enough food left for two days. Crouched in his sleeping bag with aching frozen fingers Scott wrote of those days, "I do not regret this journey which has shown that Englishmen can endure hardship, help one another and meet death with great bravery as ever in the past. Had we lived I should have had a tale to tell of the hardihood, endurance and courage of my companions which would have stirred the heart of every Englishman. We shall stick it out to the end, but we are getting weaker, of course, and the end cannot be far. It seems a pity but I do not think I can write more. What lots and lots I could tell you of this journey. How much better it has been than lounging in too great comfort at home." Wilson and Bowers were the first to die. Scott was left alone. He continued to write in his diary until the pencil dropped from his hand. His last entry, before he died, was, "For God's sake, look after our people."

A search party, eight months later, found the tent, the three bodies, the letters, and Scott's diary. Over their resting place, the search party built a cairn of stones and above it placed a simple wooden cross made of broken skis. On the cross were the names of the heroic men and these words:

To strive, to seek, to find, and not to yield.

TEST

Choose the phrase that will make the statement true:
1. Scott was   (a) an Englishman
                (b) an American
                (c) an Italian
2. His ship was the   (a) *Golden Hind*
                       (b) *Terra Nova*
                       (c) *Quest*

3. The last inhabited land he touched before sailing to Antarctica was (a) South Africa
   (b) New Zealand
   (c) South Georgia

4. The fresh meat that Scott's party ate was
   (a) penguin and seal
   (b) beaver and otter
   (c) reindeer and polar bear

5. Scott established his base camp near (a) Mount Erebus
   (b) Mount Everest
   (c) Mount Hecla

6. On the final dash to the South Pole, besides Scott there were
   (a) two men
   (b) four men
   (c) fifteen men

7. The explorer who reached the South Pole ahead of Scott was
   (a) Shackleton
   (b) Cook
   (c) Amundsen

8. On the return journey from the South Pole, Scott and his men suffered from (a) small-pox
   (b) lack of food
   (c) scurvy

9. The last member of the party to die was (a) Evans
   (b) Oates
   (c) Scott

10. Scott will be remembered for all time because
    (a) he reached the South Pole
    (b) of his great courage in the face of terrible hardships
    (c) he climbed the Beardmore Glacier

THINGS TO DO

1. On a blackboard map of the Antarctic continent mark in the route taken by Scott on his way to the South Pole. Mark in the return route also. Print in the following names in their correct locations: (a) Scott's base camp, (b) Beardmore

Glacier, (c) One-ton Depot, (d) South Pole, (e) place where Scott died.

2. Make a coloured picture of the flag which was flying at the South Pole when Scott reached it.

3. Why is pemmican of great value to explorers?

BOOKS TO READ

For the Teacher

The Book of the Long Trail, Henry Newbolt. *Longmans Green & Co. Ltd.*

Exploration and Discovery, A. Archer. *Cambridge University Press.*

For the Pupil

A Book of Discovery, M. B. Synge. *Thos. Nelson & Sons Limited.*

The Book of Discovery, T. C. Bridges. *George G. Harrap & Co. Ltd.*

The Book of Polar Exploration, E. L. Elias. *George G. Harrap & Co. Ltd.*

Boys' Book of Exploration, M. Harris Gable. *E. P. Dutton & Co.*

The Foundations of History, Book D, Part II., P. Wragge. *Thos. Nelson & Sons Limited.*

Heroes of Exploration, R. Finch. *University of London Press.*

They Went Exploring, Arensa Sondergaard. *Harper & Bros.*

RICHARD BYRD

Other explorers followed Scott, Shackleton, and Amundsen into the Antarctic. After each party returned, new coast-lines, lands, and mountain ranges were added to the map. Improved means of exploration were developed; now men could travel in hours, by aeroplanes, long distances which only a few years before would have taken many weeks to cover. Tractors could be used to pull loads much heavier than teams of dogs could haul. The invention of radio permitted men to keep more easily in touch with their headquarters.

One of the first explorers to make use of these new inventions was Richard Byrd, an officer in the American Navy. In 1926 he had made a successful flight over the North Pole; in 1927 he had flown across the Atlantic from the United States of America to France. On his return he stated that he would not be content until he had flown over the South Pole also.

For such an expedition months of careful planning and preparation were needed. Byrd began by reading everything he could find about the Antarctic, books, magazines, diaries, and charts of all kinds. Next he searched for a sturdy wooden ship which would be able to withstand the tremendous pressure of the ice-pack in the polar seas. He was fortunate in finding just the right type of ship in Norway. It was one which had, for years, battled its way through the ice-floes in the Arctic seas. This vessel had sides of a tremendous thickness, thirty-four inches of solid wood. It was re-named the *City of New York*. Later Byrd added two more ships, the *Eleanor Bolling* and a whaler, the *Larsen*. He also obtained four planes, several tractors and a wonderful radio set which was valued at $25,000. Huge supplies of gasoline and coal were amassed.

Byrd planned to carry enough supplies to care for the expedition for two years and possibly three years in case the ice closed in and prevented his return.   The following list will give some idea of the tremendous quantities of food which had to be ordered: ham, two tons; bacon, three tons; beef, five tons; pork, two tons; lamb, one ton; chicken, one ton; turkey, six hundred pounds; pork sausage, two tons; butter, two tons; and eggs, five hundred cases.   These were only a few items of the long list of foods which the ships had to carry.

On Aug. 25, 1928, the *City of New York* sailed from the city for which it was named amidst the blowing of whistles and the cheering of vast crowds of people.   Early in December, it reached New Zealand where it was joined by the two other ships.   Time and again during the next few years Byrd spoke warmly of the great help that the people of New Zealand willingly gave to him.   Last minute preparations were made there and then the three vessels headed for the Antarctic seas.

Byrd planned to make his base camp in the Antarctic near the Bay of Whales where a ship can get closer to the South Pole than at any other place.   Before reaching this bay, however, the ships had to fight their way through dangerous ice floes, pushing the cakes aside, backing up and ramming forward with great difficulty.   When the vessels reached the Bay of Whales, Byrd found that it was covered with several feet of ice, and beyond the bay, the Great Ice Barrier rose up in some places to a height of over forty feet.

The ships anchored close to the edge of the bay ice and the unloading was begun.   This was a time of great danger for Byrd and his men, for cracks were continually forming and great pieces of ice repeatedly broke off and floated out to sea.   Byrd, at all times anxious for the safety of his men,

urged them to work both by night and by day to complete
their task before the ice on which they were unloading
cracked and broke away. The base camp was established
at a safe place several miles inland and to the camp Byrd
gave the name Little America. Communication between

THE UNLOADING WAS BEGUN

ship and base was established. When a party of men with
a heavily-loaded sledge left the ship, news of the departure
was radioed to Little America and those at the camp were
on the watch for the arrival of the sledge party. Fearing
that some of the men might get lost on the way, Byrd
insisted that they carry supplies of food and sleeping-bags
with them.

At Little America huts were built. There were bunk
houses, machine shops, radio rooms, and work rooms as well
as storehouses for clothing, food, coal, and gasoline. Kennels
made out of packing-cases were prepared for the Eskimo
dogs. Radio towers were erected. Because of the great
danger of fire the buildings were placed at safe distances
from one another. Snow tunnels connected the many

buildings. The outside walls and the roofs were painted a bright orange colour so that they could be easily seen from planes.

Before winter set in several flights were made by the planes. On one flight, a plane landed many miles from the base camp and established a depot where food, clothing, coal, and gasoline were stored. A severe storm prevented the plane from returning to its base. During the storm, the plane was so badly damaged that it was a total wreck. A radio call for help was sent back to Little America. Immediately another plane was sent out and rescued the party of men. This modern invention, radio, repeatedly proved of great help and comfort to Byrd's expedition. Several journeys were made by dog teams to establish bases for food and fuel before the long Antarctic night set in and made all travel impossible.

From April until August the forty-two men left in Little America spent the hours of darkness busily preparing for the three expeditions which they hoped to make when the daylight returned once again. The first two journeys were to be long ones using sledges and dog teams and were to be made into the Queen Maud Mountains, a region about which little was known. The third journey to the South Pole Byrd hoped to make by plane.

On Saturday nights during the winter the men received and sent radio messages to the United States of America. Listeners in Canada and the U.S. could hear these messages travelling nine thousand two hundred miles in a few seconds, and opening with the words, "This is Little America calling!"

The men enjoyed the most wholesome of foods, for their diet had been carefully planned before they left America. There was plenty of variety and there was added to their usual diet, meat found in the Antarctic, whale, seal, and penguin. Whale meat was not very popular with the men for it was very strong in flavour and often very tough; the men liked it best when it was chopped up and fried with onions. Penguin meat was eaten only occasionally for the men disliked its oily, fishy flavour.

The sun returned in August and by September a skiing party left camp to establish more food depots which were

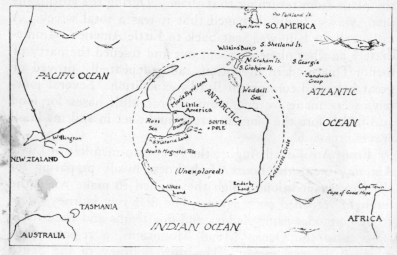

ANTARCTICA

placed about fifty miles apart along the route that a larger skiing party would take later in the season. Orange flags attached to bamboo poles were placed along the trail as guides and special markers were used to point out dangerous places where there were deep almost hidden cracks or crevasses.

In November the larger skiing party set out with ten sledges of supplies and teams of dogs. This journey was to be roughly one thousand three hundred miles in length and it would take over three months. This was the longest journey by sledge ever taken in the cause of science. When the men returned they brought back much new knowledge not only about the mountain range, but, through fossils discovered there, about plants and animals which must have, at one time, lived in the Antarctic.

Clear weather was necessary for the plane journey over the mountains to the South Pole and in the Antarctic there are very few days when the weather is favourable for flying. One day, late in November, the weatherman reported clear weather; he also said "You had better go now; another chance may not come." This was the report for which Byrd had been waiting. He prepared to take off. On this important flight he planned to be the navigator and he took three others aboard with him, a pilot, a photographer, and a radio operator. Photographs were to be taken all along the seven hundred and ninety-two mile route to the Pole and back. Byrd expected the flight to take twenty-four hours. It was of the utmost importance to carry a heavy supply of gasoline. In case his plane should have engine trouble and be forced down many miles from its base he had also to take large quantities of food. All of these supplies weighted the plane down and he wondered if it would be able to fly high enough to clear the treacherous mountain peaks over which it had to pass.

The men left behind cheered as the plane took off from Little America. Through the sky, at a speed of one hundred and five miles an hour, it roared to the south. As Byrd approached the mountains the weather was perfect but the plane, weighed down with its heavy load, refused to climb high enough to clear the peaks. Balchen, the pilot, yelled, "It's drop two hundred pounds or go back." Byrd had to decide whether he should drop that weight in gasoline or in food. He well knew that if they were forced down they would need the food but he quickly replied, "A bag of food overboard," and a month's supply of food hurtled down into the snow below. Even yet the plane was still too heavy and once again Byrd signalled that food be dropped instead of gasoline. Slowly, foot by foot, yard by yard, the plane climbed higher and higher into the air until at last all danger of crashing on the mountain peaks was over.

THE WEATHER WAS FAVOURABLE FOR FLYING

The motors sang once again and from then on, the commander knew that all would be well. No new dangers appeared. On November 29, 1929, the plane roared over the South Pole. Byrd opened a trap-door and dropped out a small bundle, the flag of the United States of America, the Stars and Stripes, attached to a small stone from the grave of Floyd Bennett, his great friend for whom the plane was named. This radio message was sent back to Little America, "We have reached the vicinity of the South Pole. Soon turn north. We are putting the Pole behind us and racing home."

Back over the snow-covered mountains the plane soared and down to the advance supply base which had been established by the ski party. There the plane was refuelled. It returned without mishap to Little America. That night Byrd wrote these words: "We were deaf from the roar of the motors, tired from the strain of the flight, but we forgot all that in the tumultuous welcome of our companions." Byrd had succeeded; in less than sixteen hours he had covered the distance that had taken the Norwegian explorer, Amundsen, ninety-seven days to make. Richard Evelyn Byrd was the only man to have made flights over both the North and the South Poles.

With their work completed, Byrd and his men prepared for home. The *City of New York* which in the meantime had made a journey to New Zealand, returned and docked along the edge of the bay ice. Hastily the supplies were packed on board and Little America was left behind as the ship headed out of the Bay of Whales.

"With nothing but open water between us and home I was able," Byrd wrote, "to wire the family of every man who had braved the fourteen months of the Antarctic expedition, that he had come through safe and sound. It was a great relief to me." At all times throughout the long months, Richard Byrd's chief concern had been for the health of his men. He had carried out all of his plans without the loss of a single man in Antarctica.

Second Voyage

Early in 1934, Byrd returned to the Antarctic. As the ships fought their way through the pack-ice to the Bay of Whales, Byrd and his men anxiously peered through their binoculars to see if Little America with its many buildings and radio towers was still standing, or if it had been destroyed by the ceaseless gales and blizzards. Straining their eyes, they saw tiny black specks in the snow. They were the tops of the towers of the radio station. Little America had endured.

When the men landed and journeyed over the snows to the deserted camp they found that the buildings remained as they had left them. They entered and found long icicles hanging from the roof. Byrd's own quarters looked like a giant's cave. His reading lamp, half full of kerosene, was there beside his bunk exactly as he had left it. Seal and whale meat which had been left hanging from the ceiling of another room was still perfectly preserved; a pot of frozen coffee was on the stove and coal was still in the bin.

Byrd planned to use Little America again as his base camp. Supplies were speedily unloaded from the ship and the tremendous task of hauling them from the ice shelf to Little America was begun. This time Byrd used tractors as well as dog sledges. The greatest of care was taken with the unloading of the planes, one a huge Condor, the pride of the expedition, and another a strange-looking flying machine, an autogiro, which the men jokingly nicknamed "The Tired Windmill".

Shortly after the establishment of the base camp a weather station was built one hundred and twenty-three miles south of the base. Here Byrd hoped to gather important information about the weather and winds in the Antarctic. His plan was for someone to go there and stay through the long winter months of darkness and keep daily records of the temperature, strength of wind, and amount of moisture in the air. Byrd knew that it would be a great strain on a man's nerves staying there all alone for many months with no company of any kind. He, himself, decided to go. For four and a half months in the year 1934 Byrd was isolated from the camp. Each day he opened the trap-door in the top of the hut, went out and took readings. His daily reports were sent by radio to Little America. The rest of his time he spent cooking meals, reading, working out problems, and listening to the radio. At times, there were gaps in the radio reports and the base camp knew that something was wrong. Twice, parties of men from Little America left the camp and tried to fight their way in the pitch darkness of the Antarctic winter over the frozen wastes to Byrd's quarters, but both times they were forced to turn back.

In the meantime, at the lonely hut, fumes from a faulty kerosene stove were slowly poisoning Byrd. He knew that the fumes were escaping and causing his illness but he could not repair the stove. No hint of this reached Little America. Meanwhile, alarmed by the gaps in the reports a tractor party from Little America set out on one of the most difficult journeys ever undertaken. In complete darkness, and fighting their way through a terrific blizzard, the rescuers finally reached their leader. They were very shocked at his appearance. Byrd was pale, weak, and hollow-cheeked. He was much too ill to be taken back to camp. He rested for some weeks regaining his strength. When his health improved a plane from Little America took him safely back to the base.

Byrd's notes, which he had carefully kept during his isolation, contained a great fund of information about temperatures, winds, moisture in the air, shooting stars, clouds, and the Southern Lights. His records showed that in the depth of winter the temperature had gone as low as eighty-three degrees below zero. In spite of his serious illness, Byrd had carried out all that he had planned to do.

After a short rest and some time before he had regained his health, Byrd set out on another expedition, this time in the big Condor plane, to find out if Antarctica was one continent, or whether a channel divided it into two land masses. On the journey the plane carried skis, tents, cookers, and sledges as well as food in case the men were forced down far from their base. The flight was successful beyond their dreams. There was no great water passage dividing Antarctica in two; they found out that it was one continent. A few days after the return of the Condor plane, another group of men set out and flew over the same region. They agreed with Byrd's findings in every way.

The autogiro, whose chief value was in its ability to land and take off from a very tiny space, was used on a few short

trips before it crashed and had to be abandoned.

When the brief Antarctic summer weather returned Byrd's ship made its way back to the Bay of Whales from New Zealand and brought back letters from

PENGUINS

home. No letters had been received for over a year. As excited as schoolboys, the homesick men raced over the snows on skis, by dog team and by tractor, to reach the long-awaited ships.

Byrd knew that Little America must be vacated with all speed for he was aware that the ice might freeze in around the ships and delay their return for another year. The work of loading was hastened and soon Byrd's men said farewell to Antarctica.

On board the ships were thirty-eight penguins which had been requested by zoos in the United States. Only a few survived the trip to America. When Byrd was received by President Roosevelt in Washington, he presented to his President a little penguin perched on a cake of ice.

TEST

Complete each sentence in Column I by choosing the suitable words or a date from Column II:

COLUMN I	COLUMN II
1. Byrd landed in Antarctica near the ——————.	(a) orange colour
2. Byrd's base camp was called ———— ————.	(b) Nov. 29, 1929
3. The outside walls and roofs of the buildings were painted an ———— ————.	(c) total darkness
4. Two fresh meats which the explorers obtained in Antarctica were ———— and ————.	(d) weather station
5. The date on which Byrd flew over the South Pole was ———— ————	(e) live penguin
6. Byrd went to Antarctica for a second time in ———— ————.	(f) Bay of Whales
7. During the second expedition, Byrd spent the winter months at a ———— ———— all alone.	(g) poisonous fumes from a kerosene stove
8. During the winter Byrd became ill because of ———— ———— ———— —— ———— ————.	(h) penguin and whale
9. Rescue parties found it difficult to reach Byrd because of the ———— ————.	(i) 1933-1935
10. On his return from this journey Byrd presented President Roosevelt with a gift from Antarctica. It was a ———— ————.	(j) Little America

THINGS TO DO

1. Plan a radio programme. Divide the class into two groups. One group will pretend they are at Little America with Byrd, the other group are friends and relatives of the explorers and are at Station KDKA in the United States of America. What messages would be sent over the air-waves?
2. Make believe that you are Richard E. Byrd. You have just returned to Little America from the flight over the South Pole on November 29, 1929. Write a letter home telling of this exciting experience.
3. If you enjoy manual training, make a model of the *Floyd Bennett,* the plane in which Byrd made his flight over the South Pole. Look up pictures of this plane in the *National Geographic Magazine* (Aug. 1930).
4. Collect clippings from newspapers and magazines of Rear-Admiral Richard E. Byrd's expedition to Little America in 1946-1947. Put these pictures and clippings up on the class bulletin board. Be sure to find a picture of Byrd.

BOOKS TO READ

FOR THE TEACHER

A History of Geographical Discovery and Exploration, J. N. L. Baker. *George G. Harrap & Co. Ltd.*

The National Geographic Magazine, Aug. 1930, Washington, D.C., U.S.A.

The National Geographic Magazine, Oct. 1935, Washington, D.C., U.S.A.

Scout to Explorer, P. Siple. *G. P. Putnam's Sons.*

FOR THE PUPILS

Boys' Book of Exploration, M. Harris Gable. *E. P. Dutton & Co.*

In Little America with Byrd, J. and O. Hill. *Ginn & Co.*

They Went Exploring, Arensa Sondergaard. *Harper & Bros.*